MASONIC AFTER-DINNER
SPEAKING

MASONIC AFTER-DINNER SPEAKING

Laurence Ager

© 1985 L. Ager
Published by Lewis Masonic
Ian Allan Regalia, Coombelands Lane,
Addlestone, Surrey KT15 1HY
Members of the Ian Allan Group

ISBN 0 85318 142X

First Published in the United Kingdom 1985
This edition 1993

British Library Cataloguing in Publication Data

Ager, Laurence
Masonic after-dinner speaking.
1. Public speaking.
I. Title
808.5'1'0243661   PN4121

ISBN 0-85318-142-X

Printed in Great Britain by Ian Allan Printing Ltd, Coombelands House, Addlestone, Surrey KT15 1HY

Contents

Foreword

It is my pleasure to introduce to Freemasons this much needed and most helpful work by W Bro Ager on the art of Masonic after-dinner speech making. We all take it for granted that in the lodge room we aim at standards of excellence and sincerity in the performance of our ritual. At the festive board we look to maintain standards of true fellowship. In both these areas we can rely on known ritual and accepted standards of conduct to guide us. But when it comes to the after-dinner speeches, we lack similar guide lines on what is expected. Each of us is forced back on to his own resources in deciding what to say and how to say it: what is relevant to the Masonic occasion, and what is irrelevant. It is in this field that the author offers much valuable guidance. He helps to show each of us how to use such talents as we possess, and posts warning notices that the object of speech making is to inform and to entertain and never to risk boring one's audience. The author teaches courage to the timid, moderation to the brash, style to those willing to learn. There is help here for every type of speaker. Let us not also forget that the majority of us are listeners and not speakers, and may well feel grateful to W Bro Ager for helping to make more tolerable what Shakespeare called 'the setting sun, the music at the close.'

LEONARD BARFORD.
Provincial Grand Master for Sussex.

CHAPTER ONE

The Elements

A tap on the shoulder during the meal, followed by a request to propose the toast to the visitors is for many a Mason an end to his enjoyment of what had promised to be a happy evening. It is a sad fact that what ought to be one of the most attractive features of Lodge after-proceedings can so often become a source of worry to the speaker and of boredom to his audience. The object of this book is to provide sufficient elementary instruction to enable any Mason to rise with some degree of confidence and to speak for the required few minutes without disgrace.

It has to be emphasised at the outset that the ability to make an effective off-the-cuff speech is possessed by very few—far fewer, I would suggest, than the number who *think* they can do it. Churchill never spoke impromptu: every speech he delivered was prepared with assiduous care.

To be effective in masonic after-dinner speaking you do not need to be a great orator, but you do require certain basic equipment which I propose to provide. A surprising number of Masons experience actual fear when asked to propose a toast. I knew one unfortunate man who rose on the summons, 'Pray silence for Brother So-and-So', and then remained transfixed and tongue-tied until the sympathetic brother beside him stood up and said the required few words on his behalf. It is not necessarily lack of courage, but rather a feeling of inadequacy which can bring this about; and the realisation that the eyes of all the brethren are upon you generates sufficient tension to make you dumb.

Some of us can remember our first ceremony as Master of a Lodge when, having sounded the gavel and risen with the words, 'Brethren, assist me to open the Lodge' the awful realisation struck us that from now on the responsibility was entirely ours. And some have suffered a mental black-out for a few seconds—a far more common experience than everyone will be prepared to admit.

It cannot be emphasised too strongly that after-dinner speaking at a masonic gathering differs quite considerably from what is expected, for example, among Rotarians, Round Tablers, or members of Lions Clubs or 41 Clubs. Many Masons belong to these excellent organisations, and they will at once appreciate the fundamental differences in outlook. These I will deal with later. It may sound trite to offer as the first and most important piece of advice that you should be yourself when speaking. Let us confess that many of us strive, when we get on our feet, to put on an act. Some even adopt an accent which is not their own. This may not necessarily come about through lack of confidence: it may be prompted by a well-meant wish to entertain—or more probably by a less laudable desire to impress. It may be expected of you in delivering half an hour's technical paper that you should know it all; but in a toast lasting a few minutes after dinner the attitude of the lecturer is out of place.

It may be that you really do consider that you are somebody of importance, and that the adoption of a bogus humility would not represent the genuine *you*. If that is so, your task will not be as easy as that of your less exalted brethren; but there is no reason why your oratory should be less acceptable, provided always that it is the real *you* that is speaking, and not the you of your imagination. It was the great Dr Samuel Johnson who enquired of an obviously pompous and self-satisfied speaker: 'Pray, sir, are you anyone in particular?'

The word 'sincerity' is vastly overdone in masonic speaking, but it is necessary to emphasise that the views you express should be sincerely held by you, unless you are introducing humour. In that case it ought to be made quite clear to the brethren that the views which have been mooted are *not* yours. It can be embarrassing when everything is over to be button-holed by an earnest brother with the question: 'Did you really mean what you said about such-and-such?' You might have to reply: 'Of course not; I was leg-pulling', at which point all the humour will have evaporated.

Humour is always welcome in after-dinner speaking, but its introduction poses one of the greatest difficulties in the art. We have all sat through speeches which consisted of two or three entirely irrelevant jokes cribbed in part from television, and consequently known to many, and giving little pleasure to anyone. We all think we can tell a story, but to do so standing on your feet and addressing an audience is not always as easy as it looks. Every funny story has a punch line at the end. How often, if sitting at any distance from the speaker, have we not entirely lost it owing to the habit which we all have (let's confess it) of dropping our voice at the end of a sentence. It is a practice which is absolutely maddening to our listeners.

The custom of introducing humour, and in particular funny stories, into masonic speech-making is valuable but beset with danger. Jokes really should have some relevance to the matter in hand. 'That reminds me of the story of—' too often introduces a tale having no possible bearing on the subject. I would give a serious warning against introducing questionable stories into masonic speeches. I have heard it said that we are all mature men, so what does it matter? 'We have no scruples in the other associations to which I belong, so why should we be so mealy-mouthed in Masonry?' The reason is that in Masonry we are a carefully selected body of men, each of whom has declared at his initiation his trust and belief in God, and his sincere wish to render himself more extensively serviceable to his fellow men. From there he has progressed through a serious study of the symbolism of birth, life and death; and in contemplating the last of these he has been taught to reflect upon that most interesting of all human studies, the knowledge of himself.

Some at least of these high-flown ideas must accompany all Masons out of the Lodge room and into the dining room. The new-made Mason in particular must surely be shocked to find the atmosphere so changed that a dirty joke which might have been acceptable among two or three men in the corner of the bar should be retailed in a speech. Such a story was related to my knowledge at the after-proceedings of an installation ceremony, resulting in the Provincial Grand Master and his entourage leaving immediately in protest. This sort of story does nothing to enhance the dignity and high importance of Freemasonry, and might well nurture the feeling among brethren that Masonry, after all, is only another club. It is well, therefore, to choose your stories with care, to avoid if possible those which must be well known to your audience, and to be aware that the point is bound to be lost if every word is not clearly audible. Hence don't hurry, bear in mind that every word has to carry, and try all you can to *project your voice*.

The advice which used to be given to actors, professional as well as amateur, was that they should, without shouting, consider themselves to be addressing the rather deaf old lady sitting in the back row of the circle. Projecting the voice is largely psychological. We automatically adopt a different tone quality when conversing at close quarters. Try it: it is quite different from the tone we employ when buying a newspaper on a crowded railway station. It is not necessary to shout, but in your mind, and consequently in your voice, you are addressing in person the brethren at the furthest distance from you. Some men have a naturally monotonous voice—a voice all on one note. This used to be common among certain members of the clergy. It is a serious disadvantage to the speaker, and despite my advice that we should all speak naturally, I feel strongly that it should be overcome. We all have more than one note in our speech: we raise our voice at the end of a question, and we tend to drop it when answering one. Key words have to be accented at a slightly higher pitch, and sympathy and compassion can be effectively conveyed lower down the scale, provided always that the result is audible.

I feel that a speaker should never turn away or bury his chin in his chest; and (dare I mention it?) you can't be heard if you don't open your mouth. It is *you* the brethren want to hear, so for goodness sake don't ask questions of the brother seated beside you. The view is often expressed: 'So long as I am understood, what the hell does it matter? We're all friends and brothers anyway.' Although in masonic after-dinner speaking we none of us regard ourselves as among the great speakers of the age, nevertheless it is only courteous to our brethren to make an effort at least to be coherent and understandable. We want to please by being our natural selves, by employing our own customary vocabulary, and by speaking intelligently and simply.

You would be surprised at how much your stance adds to the effectiveness of your delivery. Even if it is your natural position it is better not to be round-shouldered when speaking. The best stance is to stand upright and to take reasonably deep breaths. We should always remember the advice which is attributed to that great actor, Ralph Richardson, namely that the most precious things in speech are pauses. There is plenty of time and no need to hurry. And although it may be perfectly natural to you to speak with your hands in your pockets, I suggest seriously that it is not good practice while making a speech. It is distracting, to say the least, to witness fidgeting with coins and keys in trouser pockets; and you haven't a hand immediately available to make a point or to turn over your notes. It is not unknown for a speaker with his hands com-

fortably in his trouser pockets suddenly to require to make
a special point with his right hand. Out it comes together
with a flood of coins or a handkerchief—a procedure embarrassing to the speaker, even if it may prove amusing to
some of his audience.

Before getting down to the preparation and content of
the speeches you are to deliver, there are a few more tips
to be passed on. Bear in mind that once you know how,
anyone can do it. The audience is always your friend, and
it is unnecessary and indeed dangerous to stoke up on
'dutch courage'. The extra drink before you stand up may
make your ideas less clear to you than they were, and will
pretty certainly cloud them to your hearers. You may de-
lude yourself that you are doing better than you had hoped,
for we have all met the man who assures you that he
speaks better after he's had a few. The truth is that he only
thinks he does.

You may feel that it is superfluous to mention facial
expression, but it is important not to emulate the nervous
speaker who looks straight ahead, perhaps over the heads
of the brethren, with just one fixed expression on his face.
And having learned your speech, for heaven's sake don't
recite it. This is one reason why, despite advice given to
the contrary by acknowledged experts, I am not in favour
of learning a speech by heart. By all means memorise it by
going over it repeatedly beforehand, but when it comes to
delivering it, do have your notes on the table in front of
you. The memory can be capricious, and we have all seen
speakers who have gone to much trouble and have suddenly been lost for the right word. In consequence they
become stumped and confused. I saw this happen to an
unfortunate parson in a live television broadcast. In the
course of an effective two-minute address his memory
deserted him, and he had to fish in his cassock pocket for
his script. We are none of us any the worse for not belonging to that very rare breed of true impromptu speakers.
Some who wish to give the impression that their speech is

spontaneous will often be found to have memorised just one or two speeches which they trot out on all occasions, suitable and unsuitable. If you try this I can assure you that you are certain to be found out!

CHAPTER TWO

Preparing your speech

In respect of the preparation of speeches I am not laying down rules, but rather offering simple advice. So if you are taking your task seriously, start by writing every speech out in full. If you possibly can, give yourself time to do it at one sitting. The temptation is to sit down, to get some ideas, and then to jot down the odd few words—with dashes in between—as reminders. This is putting the cart before the horse, for there is a big difference in circumstances between your sitting quiet and uninterrupted at your desk, and standing up before an assembly of convivial Masons. A note such as 'Refer to innovation—paraphrase' meant something when you put it down, but your memory may or may not immediately respond. It is much more likely to respond if you have actually written down and rehearsed to yourself something like this from the new Master responding to his toast after his installation:

'Every Master hopes to leave his imprint on his Lodge, and in order to do this he must not forget his undertaking not to permit any *innovations* in the body of Masonry, no matter how trivial they may be. I should not like to promise that you will not hear from me the occasional short *paraphrase* of the ritual; but that, I assure you, will not be an innovation—it will be a quirk of my unreliable memory.'

Every speech has a beginning, a middle and an end, and there are plenty of experienced speakers who will assure you that the first and last are the most important. That great conductor, Sir Thomas Beecham was reported to have told the members of his orchestra that so long as they got the beginning and the ending right, what came in between didn't greatly matter. I have always doubted the authenticity of that story, because Beecham (although admitting that he had a 'damn bad beat') was one of the most inspired conductors of the century.

There is not a great deal of room for originality within the constricted space of masonic speech-making, so in setting out to prepare a speech I suggest that the first task is to get ideas for the middle. I shall provide some suggestions for these in their appropriate places later on. For the moment we are dealing with the mechanics of writing down. I should like to offer every possible encouragement, especially as I have been urging you to be yourself, but if I were you I would do my best not to be facetious. To some it appears clever, but it can so easily give offence.

I am never happy about 'name dropping.' It might be that the brethren would be interested in your meeting with Lord So-and-So when you went up to London to be presented with a token of appreciation from the chairman of your company; but if it has no bearing at all on the toast you are proposing or replying to, there is the possibility that your brethren (however kindly disposed) may be a little less than appreciative. A piece of advice which has been given to speakers for ages is this: if you haven't struck oil in two minutes—stop boring. It has an alternative in: As mother Whale said to baby Whale, 'If you stop spouting you won't get shot at'.

I am in favour of introducing anecdotes, but they really must have a bearing on the subject and not be introduced, as it were, out of the blue. It is unwise to put yourself into anecdotes or funny stories. We all know the ploy: 'A funny thing happened to me on the way to Lodge this evening.' Professional comedians can get away with this, but never amateur ones like you and me. If it should be that you want to mention something that really did happen on the way to Lodge, then you will have to emphasise it by something like this: 'You'll never believe it, but this really did happen to me on the way here this evening.' Even then they might not believe you!

Certain points must be borne in mind when introducing funny stories. Those picked up from television are automatically out, for they have probably been heard by your audience, and anyway it is doubtful if you can relate them as successfully as the professional comedians who first put them over. Never, as I have said before, retail dirt or anything likely to harm the susceptibilities of any of the brethren. To this end there are certain subjects which it is better to avoid altogether. Religion and politics, as we all know, are already forbidden. There are stories, too, which can give hurt or offence quite unwittingly to some brethren when such subjects are introduced as stuttering, deafness, blindness or mental instability. Irish and Jewish brethren may not always take kindly to some of the stories against them; so if a brother of either of these nationalities is known to be present it would be kind to save that funny joke for another occasion.

There is not much that you can do about the joke that falls flat, except not to risk it on any future occasion. I am not referring here to the questionable story resulting in either complete silence or a walk-out by the 'high-ups'. We all have our individual sense of humour, and what appears funny to me will not necessarily have the same impact on you. I once used the story of the man who was worried about his habit of talking to himself, so he went to see his doctor about it. His doctor said: 'Many people talk to themselves. It's quite common. Just don't worry about it.' And the man replied: 'But I *do* worry, doctor. You see, I'm such a crashing bore.' I still think it's funny, but it didn't raise a smile from my listeners. Perhaps it might provoke a laugh on some future occasion, but it is not worth risking.

An important point to bear in mind when writing your speech is this: if it is successful (and perhaps even if it isn't) you will be called upon again. It would be unwise, therefore, to put too much into one speech. You will want some of those brilliant ideas for the next time you appear before the same audience. I believe that many of the brethren who call upon me to write their speeches for them may well have exhausted their own ideas in one epoch-making speech. And, having got that off their chest, they have found themselves totally bereft of further ideas.

CHAPTER THREE

Beginnings and endings

Although all masonic after-dinner speeches should be reasonably short, it is much to be desired that the first few words should be such as to command attention. I remember many years ago attending a lecture, as one of an audience of a few hundred, on the subject of public speaking. The lecturer mounted the dais, stood there, and silently looked at us. In a matter of seconds there was utter and complete silence. The lecturer then began: 'Rule No. 1, gentlemen: first obtain complete silence.' So stand there until you do—even if the gavel has to be sounded again. It is discourteous of brethren to converse during a speech, and it is unwise (to say the least) for a speaker to try to make himself heard through it. It cannot be too strongly emphasised that even in the routine speeches which Masons are called upon to deliver, the first sentence is of tremendous importance. First of all, however, comes the formal beginning, and this is generally governed by the custom of the individual Lodge. At the dinner after an installation it is not uncommon to hear toasts prefaced with the following: 'Worshipful Master, Right Worshipful Provincial Grand Master, Very Worshipful Assistant Provincial Grand Master, Officers of Grand Lodge, Officers of Provincial Grand Lodge, Officers of London Grand Rank, Brother Wardens and brethren.' This may then be followed by a purely formal toast. There are differences of opinion on this, and I should not like to tread on anybody's toes, but my own feeling is that 'Worshipful Master and brethren' is not only more dignified, but also a more fitting prelude to what is to follow. If the Provincial Grand Master is present, and the Master is proposing the toast, he may well deem it courteous to start with 'Right Worshipful Provincial Grand Master and brethren', but otherwise the single greeting of 'Brethren' from the Master is, to my mind, adequate. We are indeed all brethren, whatever our masonic rank may be, and the use of the expression, 'Brethren all', does nothing to emphasise that.

Following this, then, the first sentence of the speech must be in keeping with the subject. The frequently encountered 'I'm afraid I'm no speaker' will not do. It may well be true, and plenty of Masons demonstrate that truth as they stumble along, but it does nothing to assist the speaker's image at the start. Nor would I unreservedly recommend opening with a funny story. A due sense of modesty is no bad thing. Wasn't it George Bernard Shaw who wrote: 'You know very well that after a certain age a man has only one speech?' To our shame it must be said that this is true of some of our brethren. So, to begin with, 'Let thy speech be short,' it says in the Book of Ecclesiasticus, 'comprehending much in few words.' You can follow this with 'I shall do my best to follow this excellent advice.' Or you might prefer to amplify the quotation with: 'They say that a *bore* is a man who, when you ask him how he is— *tells you*!'

When the newly-installed Master rises at the festive board to propose The Queen and the Craft it is difficult for him to resist the temptation to start with: 'Brethren, I rise for the first time to propose, etc.' While still using quotations perhaps the following opening might appeal: 'That much-quoted Chinese sage Confucius is reported to have said "It is better to be silent and be thought a fool, than to speak and remove all doubt". None the less, Worshipful Master, I propose, with your permission, to take up a few minutes of your valuable time in which to express etc.'

Another might go like this: 'In rising to propose ... I am

mindful of the words of an old Roman philosopher to the effect that "Wise men talk because they have *something to say*: fools talk because they *have to say something*." I do not claim to be wise, but I do have something to say.' If modesty is your strong point, you might feel disposed to start with: 'Candid friends from among the brethren have told me that I have a distinction which is shared with no other brother. It is that I am the worst speaker in the Lodge. For that reason I have taken the precaution to arm myself with notes.' Here is another modest one: 'Can you imagine what it feels like when you rise to propose a toast knowing that the response is to be made by such an accomplished speaker as . . .?'

Lord Chief Justice Goddard is reported as starting an after-dinner speech by looking fixedly around his audience and then saying: 'Some of your faces look very familiar: haven't I sentenced one or two of you?' A Lord Chief Justice might get away with that, but there are very few masonic occasions when it would be suitable. If your first sentence can represent a sudden inspiration derived from the ending of the previous speech you may find you've struck oil unexpectedly. It is not often, however, that you can bring this about and still keep the tone of the speech as you had intended. And I would not counsel too great a reliance on the advice given in an anonymous bit of dog-gerel which goes:

> Begin low, speak slow;
> Take fire, rise higher;
> When most impressed
> Be self-possessed;
> At the end wax warm,
> And sit down in a storm.

Lord Mancroft said: 'A speech is like a love affair: any fool can start one, but to end it requires considerable skill.' When proposing a health the speaker will naturally finish by calling on the brethren to be upstanding to drink the most cordial of toasts to whoever it may be. There are variants of this, but the essential point is that it should not be overlooked. Have we not all seen speakers come to the end of their speech and sit down before being hastily called back on to their feet to give the toast?

The important bit is what comes immediately before. If you have been fortunate enough to have found a striking first sentence, then a good ending can often be made by a reference back to it. Sometimes a short suitable quotation from the selection provided later in the book will be found useful. A funny story, provided it has some relevance to what has gone before, will sometimes bring the toast to a happy conclusion. There was a time when business letters used to end, not with the customary 'Yours faithfully', but with the more picturesque 'I beg to remain Your obedient servant'. Indeed, this latter may still be seen very occasionally. Either form can provide an ending for the Master's reply to his toast: something like this: 'And so, brethren, I pledge myself to do my best for the Lodge. In short, as Master, I beg to remain your most obedient servant:' or, alternatively: 'And so, brethren, I am I assure you, yours faithfully'.

In responding to a toast you will naturally repeat your expression of thanks at the end, and some speakers like too add 'And thank you for so patiently listening to me.' The great Lord Macaulay, who wrote a monumental history of England as well as a lot of poetry, used to speak at great length, and one of his contemporaries remarked of him that he had occasional flashes of silence which made his conversation perfectly delightful. You could mention this and follow it with: 'So I shall now introduce a flash of silence which, if it does nothing to add to your *delight*, will at least come as a relief! Thank you for your patience.'

Some suggested endings follow. FOR GENERAL USE something like this might be acceptable: 'It is well to bear in mind that there are two sides to every question, just as there are two sides to a sheet of flypaper. But it makes a big difference to the fly—which side he chooses. So I leave it with you, brethren, to make your choice.'

Or this: 'I apologise for my shortcomings in what I have said, and I assure you that my object throughout has been to supply you with a *happy ending*. Everyone is going to be *so glad* that my speech is over!'

This in the way of thanks: 'There is little more for me to say, except to express the hope that you are all enjoying the evening as much as I am. Having established that, let me thank you again for so cordially drinking my health.'

Here is a routine one for the reply by the Master: 'We are all busy men—even on Lodge Nights—and I'm sure you've heard enough from me. I shall content myself, therefore, with saying THANK YOU, Brother ..., for your kind words; and thank you all, brethren, for the warmth of your reception of them.'

You might find this suitable as an ending when replying for the visitors: 'Worshipful Master and brethren, thank you again for so enthusiastically drinking our health; and thank you also for so stoically facing that last and greatest trial— having to listen to me!'

Or this: 'Since I have been honoured among the visitors by being deputed to reply to their toast, I have done my best to express the appreciation we all feel of your hospitality. There is an old Chinese proverb which says: "If you bow at all, BOW LOW." I am hoping that I have bowed sufficiently low to ensure that we are all asked again.'

ON LADIES' NIGHT an effective ending can be made to the toast to the ladies by quoting Hilaire Belloc's lines given in Chapter 15 under the heading of 'Friendship' (*From quiet homes and first beginnings*), and following this with: 'With that thought of laughter and the love of friends ever present in our minds, I call upon you, gentlemen (or gentlemen and brethren, if you prefer) to be upstanding to drink a most loving toast to OUR LADIES.'

Here is another for Ladies' Nights: 'So now, Mary (the

responder to the toast), over to you—but not before I have called upon *you*, Mr President and gentlemen, to raise your glasses and drink a resounding toast to THE LADIES.'

This is a suggestion for the finish of the lady's reply: 'We've each had a lovely present, and our health has been so enthusiastically drunk that I declare we all feel better for it. There's just one more thing to say before I sit down— please may we all come again next year?'

And one more idea if you are proposing the toast to the ladies: 'At this point I feel that I ought not to delay your enjoyment for a moment longer. I know perfectly well that you are enduring *me* only as a prelude to what you are looking forward to hearing from ..., who is to make the response. Frankly, I can't blame you. So without more ado I call upon you to rise your glasses etc.'

CHAPTER FOUR

The first sentence

When you sit down to write your speech, the most difficult sentence to devise is the first one. I am setting out in this chapter some openings which will provide you with a start, and which can be altered or adapted to suit the occasion. We will begin with openings suitable for when you are proposing a toast, and here is one for almost any occasion:

> The most telling parts of a speech, I am told, are the first sentence and the last. How wonderful it would be if I could stand before you, as I do now, and give voice to some world-shattering announcement!

The next idea has been used before but will stand repetition:

> What a wonderful instrument is the human brain! It starts working the moment we are born, and only stops when we get up to make a speech!

This is a plea from the heart:

> Have you ever experienced that quietly confident and absolutely assured feeling which comes to you at the critical moment just before you fall flat on your face?

This one might come from a brother who, maybe, has seldom or never been called upon before:

> I've had plenty of advice on how to tackle my speech—including the bit you all know to the effect that I should stand up, speak up and shut up!

If you know or suspect that you are to be followed by one

of the lodge's best speakers, or by a visitor with some reputation, you might find something on the lines of the following will not come amiss:

Nothing so much improves a man's driving as the realisation that his licence has expired, and that he is being trailed by a police car. In the course of a few minutes I am to be followed by that excellent speaker, Brother ..., and I have therefore gone to no little trouble in preparing my few stumbling sentences in the hope that I shall not be utterly disgraced.

Perhaps this would appeal on a Ladies' Night:

When I was instructed—or asked—or honoured (which ever is the right word) to propose/respond it was made clear to me that my contribution to the proceedings was to come under the heading of Entertainment.

If the brother to be toasted, presumably the Master, happens to be a barrister or a solicitor, the following might be adapted:

When a mere Junior Warden rises to propose a toast in the presence of a Master who is a lawyer, it is obvious that there may be serious consequences if he does not choose his words with care.

If the Master is known for his sense of humour, and is prepared to exercise it in the speech which follows, he may find something like this to be a suitable beginning:

This is the occasion on which, whether or not I have anything of importance to say, it is expected of me that I will rise to my feet and deliver a soul-stirring oration.

It may be, as I have said before, that Ladies' night presents one of the sternest tests for after-dinner speakers. Here are two suggested openings to the toast to the ladies:

Can you imagine what it feels like to face a distinguished

gathering such as this, hopefully armed with a few compliments for the ladies, and knowing that you are to be followed by so talented and beautiful a lady as . . .?

I don't suppose that all the ladies present will be *young* women, but I am confident that you will be forgiven for including them all in that category:

The late Seymour Hicks, a great actor, gave it as his considered opinion that two of the greatest joys in life are *old wine* and *young women*. Whatever your taste may be in old wine is of no interest to me: my concern this evening is with young women.

Here are a few suggestions for suitable beginnings when you are replying to a toast. The man who has to do this, most often is the Master, so here goes:

I know Brother . . . so well that there is a feeling almost of embarrassment in trying to acknowledge at all adequately the virtues which he has attributed to me.

Here is another beginning on the same theme:

I'm not quite sure whether . . .'s entirely delightful speech proposing my health is to be regarded as the truth, half the truth, or nothing like the truth.

Or you could try this:

In replying to Brother . . .'s witty speech proposing my health, I must confess to feeling rather like the patient at the dentist's who only opens his mouth when he has nothing to say.

It would be better to save this for the occasion when you follow a speaker who has some reputation:

It takes a degree of courage to make a suitable reply to such an eminent and respected speaker as the proposer of the toast.

This might well prelude the Master's reply to his toast at the dinner on Installation Night:

> It has been said that life has three great difficulties. The first is to *win* a reputation, the second to keep it while you live, and the third to preserve it after you die. Having listened to Brother ...'s kindly flattery, I might be forgiven for thinking that I have a good reputation, and the question therefore arises as to how I *keep it* after my brief year of glory is ended.

Here is another for the Master with a sense of humour:

> We sang in Lodge: 'Now the evening shadows closing Warn from toil to peaceful rest.' If there should be any brethren present who feel they would benefit from a short spell of peaceful rest—now is their opportunity.

When replying for the guests here is a self-effacing start:

> After the Lord Mayor's Show, they say, comes the dust cart. After Brother ...'s brilliant speech toasting the guests I now find myself in the position of that useful, if utilitarian, vehicle.

CHAPTER FIVE

The toast to the Initiate

This is the most important toast of the evening. Its content might well influence the initiate's whole outlook on the Order of which he has just become a member. It is essential, therefore, that without being unduly solemn, the speaker proposing his health should eschew any attempt at frivolity. The odd allusion to the new-made brother's work or interests makes the speech a more personal matter. For example I once prefaced the proposal of the toast to an initiate who happened to be a dentist with the words: 'Just sit back and relax; this isn't going to hurt you a bit.' This was followed with something like this: 'I regard it as an honour to be asked by the Worshipful Master to propose the health of our new-made brother.' This could be followed with:

'In extending the most cordial of welcomes to Brother ... I should like to draw his attention to certain matters in which (to use a phrase from his initiation ceremony) "we are distinguished from the rest of the world." In being *made a Mason* Brother ... has in effect started a new life. You cannot un-make a Mason. Even if a new-made Mason should decide (which God forbid) that he will go no further, he remains until his dying day a Mason. We take some pride in the fact that in this Lodge we exercise a proper care in the selection of those men with whom we wish to share our work, and whom we wish to become our brothers.

'This title of BROTHER is no empty word, debased

though it may have become in certain contexts. Consider for a moment the Three Grand Principles on which the Order is founded—Brotherly Love, Relief and Truth. Brotherly Love means quite literally what it says; and as our brother progresses through the next two Degrees in the Craft he will on his way undertake further obligations to his brethren, not only in this Lodge but all over the world. This is no one-way system, for in this Craft of Masonry all we who are his brethren, of no matter what race or creed, are in like manner bound to hold ourselves similarly obligated to him.

'The second great principle, that of Relief or Charity, has been demonstrated in Lodge, and in due course our Charity Steward will discuss with Brother ... the best method of discharging his obligations to the benevolent side of our work. Our brother will learn of what we do in the care of the elderly, of orphaned boys and girls, and of our wonderful hospital. Thirdly, TRUTH as between brethren, and as between brethren and the rest of the world, means exactly what it implies and admits of no doubt.

'Our new-made brother will have gathered from the Charge which was delivered by his proposer, Brother ..., that there are two subjects on which controversy in the Lodge or at the after-proceedings is absolutely forbidden, namely politics and religion. We all know how much discord can be caused by the first; and as to the second it is sufficient to quote from the First Charges of a Mason as follows: "Let a Mason's religion or mode of worship be what it may, he is not excluded from the Order, provided he believe in the Glorious Architect of Heaven and Earth, and practice the sacred dictates of morality."

'Why, then, do we become Masons? Could it not be that we feel that Freemasonry enables us to ground our relationships with *all* our fellow men on a firmer, more understanding and more compassionate foundation than

would otherwise have been the case? The greatest good
I can wish for Brother ... is that in which all the brethren
will gladly join, namely that Masonry will afford him all
that it has given us—pleasure, instruction, and the opportunity to serve our fellow men. Worshipful Master
and brethren, I give you the toast—Brother....'

You might consider that speech to be on the lengthy side,
and perhaps you would feel that reference to the charities
could better be deferred until a later occasion. Incidentally,
I have a personal dislike of the expression, 'Brother Initiate.' It seems to me that, having been made a member of
our Order, our new-made brother is entitled to be called
Brother Smith, or Jones, or Robinson straight away—just
like the rest of us.

Here is another suggestion for a toast to the initiate:

'There can be few happier occasions in Masonry than
that of welcoming a new brother. Brother ..., we do this,
every one of us, from the bottom of our hearts. You are
now a member of an institution which has for its principal object the betterment of mankind in general. We
are a world-wide brotherhood, the philosophy of which
is based upon Brotherly Love, Relief and Truth. I must
tell you now that your admission to our Order was not
made without due enquiry as to your fitness, for which
your proposer and seconder agreed to be responsible.

'We are, as you see, a Fraternity of Free and *Accepted*
Masons. You have already been taught that Freemasonry
is a peculiar system of morality, veiled in allegory and
illustrated by symbols. It is unfortunate that the word
"peculiar" should have largely changed its meaning over
the 200 years or so since the present ritual came into
being. We now tend to use the word in the sense of
something odd or strange, but the meaning in the ritual
is of something belonging exclusively to oneself. So we
do claim for Freemasonry a moral system confined to
Freemasons—a body of which you, Brother ..., are now
a member.

'You have been enjoined in the Charge (so excellently expounded by Brother ...) that in addition to the duty which you owe to the Great Architect of the Universe, you will also be exemplary in the discharge of your civil undertakings, notably in your dealings not only with your fellow Masons but also with mankind at large. In return for all this you have today forged a link with the whole body of Regular Masonry throughout the world. All its members are truly your brothers; and as you progress through the future Degrees you will, I am sure, learn to appreciate the fundamental truths upon which the whole edifice is raised. And as time goes on you may come to bless the day on which, in such a great institution, you were made a brother.'

If the initiate should happen to be a builder or an architect some reference to the influence of his particular trade or profession on the beginnings of Freemasonry could be made with advantage. Something like this might be included in his toast:

'In the Middle Ages a Mason was neither more nor less than a stonemason or builder who was recognised as being qualified in his craft. Mainly illiterate, and therefore unable to produce documents to attest to his personal skills, he was entrusted with certain words and signs as he proceeded from the rank of apprentice to that of master. These words and signs were to be guarded with the greatest care—not only for his own safety, but also for that of the brethren with whom he would be working. We who are engaged in *speculative* Masonry retain this usage in memory of our *operative* brethren of centuries ago.'

There is so much which one would like to explain to the initiate on his entry into the Craft, but it should be borne in mind that there will be opportunities later on, and that for the present it is best to keep everything reasonably simple. I put this forward as a purely personal preference, and it doubtless sounds unreasonable in Lodges where the practice has grown up, but I am not happy about the comparatively recent custom of referring to brethren in Lodge or at the after-proceedings by their first names preceded by the title of 'brother'. 'Brother Jim' and 'Brother Charlie' lack the dignity which is attached to 'Brother Smith' or 'Brother Jones', however much the titles may appear to gain in fraternal affection. If it is required to use first names at the after-proceedings, does not 'Jim' or 'Charlie' sound better without the prefix of 'Brother'?

If it is felt that the suggestions for a toast to the initiate which I have given above are a bit too solemn, here is one in a slightly lighter vein:

'Few ceremonies have given me as much pleasure as the one in which we have all joined in Lodge, and this sentiment is, I feel sure, shared by all the brethren. I have known our new-made brother for ... years, and I can consequently commend him to the brethren with every confidence. The act of introducing a man into Freemasonry signifies that his sponsors think highly of his integrity, and that they sincerely believe that he will honour the principles of Brotherly Love, Relief and Truth.

'Any do-it-yourself enthusiast will be familiar with the working tools of an Entered Apprentice although it is doubtful whether it would have occurred to him that he could apply those tools to his morals. Although it is too often debased in certain contexts, the masonic title of "Brother" really does have a serious import. In connection with the Order of which Brother ... has today become a member I would remind him that Brotherly Love means that fraternal bond which unites all the brethren in the Lodge with all other regularly initiated Masons everywhere. Perhaps even at this early stage it is prudent to mention that there exist certain irregular bodies calling themselves Freemasons. These are the ones that get into the news, but this is neither the time nor place to go into their existence.

'As our new-made brother progresses in the Craft he will be called upon to undertake further obligations to his brethren everywhere. He will be reminded that all the brethren have undertaken similar obligations to him. He is unlikely to forget the manner in which the tenet of Relief or Charity was demonstrated in Lodge. I sometimes feel sympathy with the candidate over this, and then I recollect that this is the way in which Charity has been demonstrated for more than a couple of centuries. In due course our Charity Steward will discuss with our brother the best method by which he can discharge his obligation to the important benevolent side of our work.

'As one who knows Brother ... well, I feel confident that as he progresses in Masonry he will find that his contacts with all his fellow-men (and not only his masonic brethren) will develop on a more fraternal and understanding basis. This is the confident hope of all of us who have today become his brethren, and who welcome him whole-heartedly to our numbers. Brethren, I give you the toast, etc.'

It is to be taken for granted that every toast to an initiate ought to be tailored to the individual's known tastes. It is not wise to trot out the same speech for every initiate who comes along. It will be new to the initiate but stale to the brethren. It will not, for example, be acceptable to lard with latin tags the welcome extended to a candidate who can make nothing out of them. Such a candidate as a schoolmaster, a university professor or an author might appreciate a reference which he could locate. But don't overstep yourself, because before going home your candidate may want to discuss with you the context of what you have quoted. This toast might suit such a candidate:

'There is no happier occasion in Masonry than the welcoming into the Craft of a new-made brother, for the term "Brother" is, I assure him, no empty word. Our new-made brother has been instructed in Lodge in the symbolism of the Working Tools of an Entered Apprentice, and has been recommended to spend at least some part of each working day in the contemplation of God and the service of his brethren, not necessarily masonic. He has been exhorted to treat his daily contacts with honesty, and to have regard to the benefits of education. The three main tenets of our Order are Brotherly Love, Relief (or Charity) and Truth.

'In Freemasonry we have a meeting place where all differences between man and man are subordinated to that brotherly love in which we all share. Every brother becomes either a strong support to this edifice, or else a faulty stone which could endanger the stability of the whole. Although we respect and honour other associations with not dissimilar motives, we, as Masons, give a solemn undertaking such as no other Order does. We pledge ourselves in respect of every one of our brethren, wherever dispersed over the face of land or water, and no matter to what Lodge in regular masonry he may belong, that we will welcome him as a brother, and that we will support him in all his laudable undertakings. Brother ... will perhaps remember that he was told soon after his entry into the Lodge that masonry contained great and invaluable privileges. These privileges are not the signs, tokens and words referred to in the obligation. Rather are they the secrets we keep locked up in the safe repository of our hearts—the hidden thoughts we seldom talk about except, perhaps, to those of our brethren who share with us a sympathetic interest in the deeper problems of life.

'There are some lines by the poet Browning which I should like to quote on the third tenet of Truth:

> Truth is within ourselves. It takes no rise
> From outward things, whate'er you may believe.
> There is an inmost centre in ourselves
> Where truth abides in fullness

'Thus, sustained by the fraternal affection of our brethren, supported by their charitable help and relief, and upholding the principles of undeviating truth, we are enabled to demonstrate to the world at large the proof of being a Mason. Worshipful Master and brethren, I give you the toast, etc.'

CHAPTER SIX

The toast to the Master

The toast to the Worshipful Master is the prerogative of the Immediate Past Master, and it is seldom submitted by any other brother. It is not the easiest of toasts to propose, and although much of the content must of necessity be formal, the toast gains much in effect if it can be made to contain material which is personal to the master to whom it is addressed. Reference to his profession, to his interests outside the Lodge, any sports in which he indulges, his artistic or musical proclivities, anything notable about his family or forbears—these are examples of things which might with advantage be introduced to give the toast a personal flavour.

Kindly reference to the master's progress towards the Chair is almost obligatory on the occasion of his installation, and if, on the way, he should have distinguished himself in any particular office (such, for example, as the presentation of the Explanation of the Tracing Boards, or the taking over of another office at short notice) a reference to this will give him the warm feeling that his prowess has not been forgotten.

It is as well to bear in mind that the Immediate Past Master will be making this speech at each subsequent meeting of the Lodge for the next twelve months, and if his Lodge should be one of those which meets eight times a year, he will have his work cut out to find something different to say on each occasion. My own feeling is that fulsome flattery is best avoided. Let us acknowledge that some of us are better at the ritual than others; some of us are blessed with better memories and greater confidence than others; some have approached the Chair joyfully as the fulfilment of an ambition; others have felt something approaching dread. But we have all determined to do our best; and most of us, after the opening minutes of our first ceremony, have thoroughly enjoyed the experience. It cannot be emphasised too often that if the Master has not carried out the ceremony in Lodge in the manner which one has come to expect—if, for example, his requiring much prompting has led to embarrassment—my own feeling is that reference to this ought not to be made in the after-proceedings. One has sometimes heard an Immediate Past Master with the kindest possible of motives make a sympathetic excuse or explanation. The right person to make such an excuse, if he wishes to, is the Master himself. He may have had business worries, illness at home, all sorts of reasons, but he is the man to explain if, as I have said, he wishes to.

If, unfortunately, the work from the Chair had been less than perfect, it would be totally wrong for the Immediate Past Master in his toast to refer to 'the excellent work of our Worshipful Master in upholding the high traditions of the Lodge.' Consider that this might be looked upon by the Master as sarcasm, particularly if it were to evoke a sly smile from any of the brethren. Sarcasm can be extremely cruel, and should never under any circumstances be indulged in, no matter what the provocation may be. Some men consider sarcasm to be clever. Generally it is wounding.

It will be seen that it is not easy to provide a ready-made speech suitable to toast any and every Worshipful Master. In my capacity as a speech writer I have sometimes been asked to provide a series of toasts to the Master covering his year in the Chair. Before getting down to writing these I have always wanted to know something about the Master—his job, his likes and dislikes—and also, of course, all I can about the Immediate Past Master who is proposing the toast. It is also helpful to know what ceremony will be worked at each meeting, and whether there might be any special connection between the Master and the candidate. Sometimes a Lodge meeting may fall on a certain well-known date, national or local, and this could provide material for a topical opening. As an example, here is an opening for a Lodge holding its meeting on the 1st of January: 'I can think of no better way of celebrating New Year's Day than by holding a Lodge on it.' Or for the 5th of November: 'Until this evening I had always regarded Bonfire Night as a rather pointless celebration. To-night, however, it achieves importance for all of us, for we celebrate the installation of our Worshipful Master. If he cares to regard the bonfires as being lighted in *his* honour, rather than in condemnation of a certain Guy Fawkes, none of us would disagree with him.'

The speeches which I offer as examples will almost certainly require alteration or amendment to fit individual circumstances. They are designed to include the customary sentiments: and, by the way, are contrary to what you may hear in certain quarters, the Master does not reign, he *rules*. Consequently the expression which is sometimes used with reference to the visiting masters at an installation is 'Ruling Masters', not 'Reigning Masters'.

This is a suggestion for the toast to the Worshipful Master on the occasion of his installation; given by the IPM:

As I rise for the first time to propose the health of our Worshipful Master the thought occurs to me that my position is not unlike that of a man who has been climbing a ladder, and who, having reached the top, turns round to lend a hand to the man who has been climbing up behind him. Our new master has followed in my footsteps in our progress through the various offices in the Lodge, not unlike the page in that favourite Christmas Carol, 'Good King Wenceslas'. You will remember the carol goes: 'In his master's steps he trod, Where the snow lay dinted.' Let me say at once that there has never been any *snow* in our relationship. Brother ... has now be-

come Worshipful. He is our Master, and it is my happy
duty to sit on his left and provide the occasional bit of
prompting if this should be required. From the standard
of efficiency which our Master has displayed on his way
through the offices, I think it is extremely unlikely that I
shall be overworked.

After all, brethren, you have heard quite enough of *my*
voice during my year of office, and I am sure you will
find the dulcet tones of our new Worshipful Master a
welcome change. Furthermore, it will be nice to hear
them coming from the East instead of from the West. So,
Worshipful Master, we all wish you a very happy and
successful year in the Chair, and we pledge ourselves to
a faithful discharge of our duties to you and to the
Lodge. Brethren, I give you the toast, etc.

Here is another suggestion for a toast to the Master on
the occasion of his installation:

The pleasure which I experienced in installing our
Worshipful Master in the Chair is only exceeded by the
happiness I have in proposing his health. It is unnecessary for me at this stage to dilate upon his virtues, for
they are already well known to all of us. One of the most
attractive points in Freemasonry is that in nearly every
Lodge the Master comes up from the ranks, so that by
the time he becomes 'Worshipful' he is known to be
thoroughly worthy of that title.

The brethren will know that Freemasonry owes its
origin to the ancient Trades Guilds, each of which was
ruled over by a master whose duty it was to care for all
his brethren. Symbolically this is the duty of every master
of every Lodge. He has to care for his brethren both
inside the Lodge and outside. Our new Master follows
in a long line of worthy Past Masters. Among these, I,
as the latest, consider myself the least worthy. Nevertheless, Worshipful Master, let me assure you that from my
place on your left I shall do my best to rack my memory

for any odd pieces of ritual which may not immediately spring to *your* mind. At the same time I shall have complete confidence that your reliance on my co-operation will not be misplaced. That confidence springs from the knowledge that, to judge by your work in the Lodge hitherto, you are unlikely to expect very much of me!

All your officers pledge themselves to work diligently for the good of the Lodge and of Freemasonry in general. Your sun having set in the West as Senior Warden, has now risen in the East as Worshipful Master—thus to open and enliven the day, and enable you to employ and instruct the brethren. In carrying out this injunction we all wish you a happy and successful year of office. Brethren, I call upon you to be upstanding and to drink an enthusiastic toast to our Worshipful Master.

The run-of-the-mill every-meeting toast to the Master provides, as I have implied, less scope for originality, but it does give an opportunity, where this is appropriate, to mention the ceremony which has been worked in Lodge. The Immediate Past Master must naturally be careful not to poach on the preserves of a brother who is to propose the health of the candidate. He should also bear in mind that *explicit* references to the ritual, even though the dining room doors are closed, are best avoided.

The following further ideas may be found of service when toasting the Master in the course of his year:

It is always a pleasure to rise to propose the health of the Worshipful Master, although I must confess that, as the months go by, that pleasure is tempered with some apprehension as to what I should say. There is a degree of comfort, Worshipful Master, in the thought that you too (when your time comes to assume my mantle of Immediate Past Master) will find yourself in a similar predicament. I assure you that it is not that I can find nothing to praise in your work. On the contrary, I feel that I have said it all before. This, I tell myself, is no reason why I shouldn't yet again assure you of the affectionate and fraternal regard in which you are held It always strikes me that it is particularly pleasant to be praised in the presence of one's friends and brethren. It is easy to praise you, Worshipful Master, because (if I may say so) you are the sort of man you can't help liking for the reason that *you* like your fellows.

If you look up the word MASTER in the dictionary you will find it defined as 'One thoroughly acquainted with, and skilled in, a craft.' The word WORSHIPFUL is likewise defined as 'Deserving of worship'. Both definitions are suited to you. But however skilled you may be in the Craft, you will probably agree with me that you too went through that experience which all of us who are Past Masters will immediately recognise. At your first ceremony (if I am not mistaken) you sounded your gavel and said, 'Brethren, assist me to open the Lodge'—after which it came over you that from then on it was all yours. And that was followed by the thought, 'So I'd better get it right!' As we all know, you *did* get it right, and you've continued to do so ever since. So, brethren, I call upon you, etc.

Or this:

'As I rise to propose the health of our Worshipful Master, I hope he will forgive me if I draw his attention to a passage from the ceremony with which he was installed. In the Address to the Brethren he was reminded that he, in common with all of us, should have one aim in view: to please each other and unite in the grand design of being happy and communicating happiness. It was further recommended that brotherly love and affection should always distinguish us as men and as Masons.

'We have all experienced our Worshipful Master's willingness at all times to promote fraternal harmony within the Lodge, and we have no doubt that in his visits to other Lodges he acts as our most worthy ambassador.

I deplore flattery, but it is only right and just that credit should be given where it is due. Our Master was instructed at his installation that he should charge all of us who are his brethren to practice out of the Lodge those duties we have been taught in it. In that way we should prove to the world the happy and beneficial effects of our ancient institution. I suggest, brethren, that we could in this have no more efficient and conscientious a mentor than our Worshipful Master, whose appreciation of the deep truths of Masonry is a model to us all.

In addition to these virtues it is but right that I should mention our Master's actual work in the Lodge. It is said that a man can only be happy in his daily work if he fulfils three requirements: he must first be fit for it; next he must not do too much of it; and finally he must have a sense of success in it. Certainly our Master is well fitted for his role as leader. As to not doing too much of it, I don't suppose that he spends so much time on Masonry that he has no leisure for anything else. And as to having a sense of success in his work, it is here that he reaps the reward of his labours in the acclaim of his brethren.

This is a suggestion for a toast in a rather lighter vein:

As I rise to propose the health of our Worshipful Master I reflect that the difficulty about this pleasant duty, however one may enjoy carrying it out, is not so much in finding virtues to extol, but rather in discovering some fresh way in which to praise those virtues with which we are all familiar.

At his installation he undertook to be a good man and true, and strictly to obey the moral law. So far as we know, that describes him exactly. Added to that, he's a peaceable subject and conforms (more or less peaceably as occasion demands) to the laws of the country in which he resides. He also submits, so far as I know, to the decisions of the supreme legislature. In addition to all that, he works diligently, lives creditably and acts

honourably by all men. His work in Lodge is so good
that none of us has to explain to our guests that slight
variations in the words are not due to lapses of memory,
but are in line with the immemorial custom of the Lodge.

Worshipful Master, we all appreciate the lead which
you give us; and from your opening words in which you
demand our assistance in opening the Lodge, right
through to the final invitation to join in the closing ode,
we are all with you and anxious to do our best. We wish
you good health and happiness during the remainder of
your year of office, and we assure you of our most willing obedience. Brethren, I call upon you to rise to drink
a toast which is worthy of the ... (many) years during
which our Lodge has worked and flourished. The Worshipful Master.

This is a variant of the above toast, to be delivered, of
course, by the Immediate Past Master:

The task, at each meeting, of preparing a toast to the
Worshipful Master is not made easier by my inability to
find in him fresh virtues to which I have not already
called attention. If only he would in the course of a
ceremony go wildly astray it would provide me with the
chance to explain why, and even possibly give me the
opportunity to point out (for the benefit of the guests)
that anyway his usage was in accordance with tradi-
tional custom. Whatever the error or omission might have
been, you could rely on the fact that whoever was down
to reply for the guests would regard it as an absolute
godsend.

As it is, our Worshipful Master leaves me no option
but to continue to praise him. I even have to repeat from
time to time my regret that I have so little to do in the
matter of prompting him! I do not wish to embellish the
words from the ceremony of your installation, Worshipful
Master, but I would suggest with great sincerity that
under your guidance we have indeed had one aim in

view: to please each other and unite in the grand design of being happy and communicating happiness.

Much of the credit for the success of our Lodge over the years is due to a long and distinguished line of outstanding masters. Not least in these ranks, Worshipful Master, there comes yourself. We hope you will long remember with pleasure your year in the Chair. For our part, we who are your brethren will look upon your year as one of the happiest in the history of the Lodge. Brethren, I call upon you to be upstanding and to drink the most cordial of toasts to our Worshipful Master.

CHAPTER SEVEN

Replying to the toast to the Master

The toast to the master is by custom laudatory, and in replying to it most of us would wish to adopt a certain modesty. The last thing we would wish would be to appear pretentious or pleased with ourselves. We may well be rather proud to have attained the Chair, but to my mind a certain seemliness is called for in replying to the toast which has been proposed by our predecessor, and honoured with enthusiasm not only by the brethren in the Lodge who are of lower masonic rank, but also by officers of Grand Lodge, Provincial Grand Lodge and London Grand Rank who may happen to be present.

The speech which gives the master most trouble is the one required of him after his installation ceremony. This is the occasion when the Lodge is on show, and is therefore required to do its best in the matter of after-dinner oratory. Purely domestic references are better reserved for subsequent meetings. On this particular occasion it is better and safer to follow certain guide lines, and not to make exaggerated references to the work you look forward to doing. Few of us make much in the way of sacrifices in doing the job of master, and let us confess that it can come (if we wish) to each of us in turn. Having listened to much high-falutin pomposity from newly-installed masters, who may have taken very seriously the address made to them in Lodge, I would recommend that any references to rewards in the after-life for meritorious service in the Chair might well be eschewed.

The proposer must, of course, be thanked, and so must

the brethren for their response. The sense of honour in the appointment, and an undertaking to do one's best, must not be omitted. The examples which I am providing represent the nucleus of most replies, and should be added to or embellished to suit the circumstances of the occasion. Suitable anecdotes could (if felt called for) be added; but as I have previously indicated, any story must have a real reference to what has been, or is about to be said. Quotations from the selection provided later in the book may be more suitable and more effective than a not-quite-suitable funny story. Reference can be made to the honour conferred by the attendance of the Provincial Grand Master or other dignitaries, but care must be taken not to steal the thunder of any brother who has been deputed to deal toast-wise with this.

Here are some ideas for the newly-installed master who, by the way, will not omit to include the visiting high-ranking officers at the start. Thus: 'Right Worshipful Provincial Grand Master, Officers of Grand Lodge, Officers of Provincial Grand Lodge and brethren.' If the Provincial Grand Master or his deputy should not be present, my personal feeling is that opening with the single word 'Brethren' is much to be preferred to the rigmarole sometimes heard, sounding like a catalogue and occasionally provoking meaningless applause. Here is a suggestion for a response which might be acceptable:

I rise for the first time—not to enquire whether any brother has aught to propose for the good of Freemasonry, but to say a heart-felt THANK YOU to you all for your reception of the toast so admirably proposed (if I may say so) by Brother.... I used the expression, 'For the first time', because in the natural order of things I shall be similarly replying on ... more occasions. I will not deny that the prospect fills me with apprehension. It has been traditionally reported of a nervous speaker that he began his speech with: 'When I arrived here only God and I knew what I was going to say. *Now* only God knows!'

However daunting may be the task of following Brother ... into the Chair, I am greatly comforted by the thought that, instead of facing him across the Lodge, I shall have his presence on my left; and that he will ever be ready with the occasional prompt if my unreliable memory should let me down. Brethren, I thank you sincerely for the honour done me in electing me as your Master, and I truly appreciate the skilful work of the Installing Master and of his whole team in carrying out the ceremony. I look forward to doing my best during my year of office to uphold the high standards of the Lodge, and to that end I rely on the regular attendance of all the brethren. As to my officers, I should like to say that my confidence in them is unbounded. I am sure that the wardens and I will make a harmonious trio, and together we shall do our best to promote that happy and fraternal spirit which has for so long been the distinguishing characteristic of our Lodge.

The following might well come fairly early on in the career of a newly installed master:

My first and most pleasant duty is to offer to Brother ... my sincere thanks for so flatteringly proposing my health. Next I have to say how grateful I am to you all, brethren, for appearing to agree with what he said! In return I promise you that I shall do my best to be a worthy follower in the steps of the distinguished masters who have preceded me.

I feel that in Freemasonry, as in other walks of life, we tend to concentrate our attention on whether Brother A. has done as well as Brother B., when the only really valid question is whether Brother A. has done *as well as he could*. I am mindful of the promise which I have made in Lodge, namely that I would do my best to secure obedience to our excellent rules and regulations; and in doing so that I would conscientiously discharge my duties as Master of the Lodge. I am well aware, brethren, that all this is rightly taken for granted by you. But we are all small cogs in the great wheel of Freemasonry, and while we are capable of doing our individual part to make the mechanism run smoothly, we are nevertheless equally capable of jamming up the works!

Let us, therefore, do our best to propagate the principles of Masonry among ourselves, while at the same time extending the tenets of Brotherly Love, Relief and Truth among those of our friends who may wish to join us from the uninstructed and popular world. So, with the fraternal co-operation of my excellent team of officers, I pledge myself to work for the spirit of fraternal happiness for which our Lodge has been for so long renowned.

After ordinary meetings of the Lodge, the Master's reply, like the proposer's toast, ought to be short. Unlike the response after the installation, its sentiments ought also to be domestic and topical. The suggestions which follow are intended to provide material which will mix with other matters which the Master may wish to mention.

In thanking you for your generous response to the toast, I should like to draw your attention to the second of the three tenets of Freemasonry: Relief or Charity. Charity, as we all know, is the distinguishing characteristic of a Freemason's heart, and most of us (I suppose) pay our dues under Deeds of Covenant. Some of these have been running unaltered for a very long time, during which the value of money has steadily fallen. May I put it to you, brethren, as a matter for consideration whether you might feel it opportune to update your charity contributions in line with something approaching the pound's present value? Brother ..., our Charity Steward will, I feel sure, be greatly interested in the result of your deliberations!

And now let me try to return the compliments which my Immediate Past Master has been showering on me, by expressing my appreciation of all he does for *me*. It is fortunate that when he has to supply the occasional word from his seat on my left we do not resemble the unlucky couple of whom the master was deaf in his *left* ear, and the I.P.M. was deaf in his *right* one. In such circumstances you could reach the stage where a puzzled initiate could be uncertain as to who was prompting whom! Of Brother ... I would say that he really *lives* his Masonry, and that Brotherly Love, Relief and Truth have ever been his personal characteristics.

Please do not think that I am founding a mutual admiration society, but I do believe in giving honour where honour is due.

If the Master or the I.P.M. have any interest in music, the following might be welcomed:

The great conductor, Sir Thomas Beecham, once said: 'There are only two things requisite so far as the public is concerned for a good performance. That is for the orchestra to *begin together* and *end together*. In between it doesn't matter much.

In thanking Brother ... for his kind words, and you, brethren, for your endorsement of them, I am tempted to wonder whether Sir Thomas's views might possibly be applied to some Lodge meetings. Certainly we are all together in the opening and closing odes, and so far as *we* are concerned what comes in between really *does* matter. This provides me with an opportunity to pay tribute to my hard-working and efficient team of officers, each and every one of whom has done his best to ensure a sincere and dignified rendering of the ceremony in which we have all taken part.

No matter what our age may be when we enter Masonry, there can be no doubt that if the three ceremonies are well carried through, they cannot do other than make a firm and lasting impression on a new-made brother. There is a distinct advantage to be gained by entering the Craft when young, not the least being that it is easier to memorise the ritual at an early age. So, while we

naturally exercise discrimination in the matter of whom
we admit and whom we decline, there is much to be
said for the encouragement of reasonably young candidates. Furthermore, the younger candidates stand a
chance of achieving higher office such as Provincial or
London Rank, or even Grand Lodge, before they are too
old to do the rank all the credit they would wish. This is
just a thought, brethren, which you might care to turn
over during the coming months before we meet again.
During that period, enjoy your holidays and have a
happy summer.

This may also provide some material on a lighter note:
It is expected of the Master of every Lodge that he will
spend some part of his time in addressing the brethren.
As I understand it, one of the masonic virtues is MERCY,
the quality of which (you will remember from Shakespeare) 'is not strained: it droppeth as the gentle rain
from heaven upon the place beneath.' I propose to exercise this virtue by being mercifully brief. To this end I
should like to thank you, Brother ... and all the brethren
in the fewest words I can decently muster.

I must confess that I take a certain pride, in company
with my officers, in doing my work as well as I am able.
And that calls to mind another passage from Shakespeare:
'There's nothing so becomes a man as modest stillness
and humility.' We are admonished in the ritual that brotherly love and affection should ever distinguish us as
men and as Masons. This is surely one of the most important of the tenets of our profession. It in no way in-
hibits us either from the enjoyment of our ceremonies, or
from the more lighthearted happiness of the after-
proceedings. The further I progress in Masonry the more
grateful I feel to the two brethren who sponsored my
admission to the Craft. For, as we all know, Masonry is
very far from being a mere dining club. To those who
pursue it steadfastly it becomes a way of life.

CHAPTER EIGHT

The toast to the Visitors

This toast provides considerable scope for the enterprising speaker. It also supplies unparalleled opportunities for the commission of bloomers. If you are going to mention any visitor by name, do be certain that you not only have his name correctly, but also its pronunciation. As to his personal likes and dislikes it is not always safe to rely on the uncorroborated information of other brethren. Since the speech can range wider than those which have preceded it, you could find it possible to introduce some of the material you have collected in the way of anecdotes, quotations, press cuttings and the like—all of which are referred to in another chapter.

The guests will already have been officially welcomed in Lodge, and so the toast after dinner will be in the nature of an extension of such a welcome. Whereas in Lodge it was hoped that they would have a happy and profitable evening, by the time this toast arrives that evening will be practically over. At this stage, then, the hope has to be voiced that they have not been disappointed. There used to be a custom in some lodges of having more than one speaker to propose the toast to the visitors, with anything up to three being called upon to reply. It is sincerely to be hoped that this practice has now come to an end. Although I am called upon to write individual speeches for brethren to deliver, I feel that in some quarters there is far too much speechmaking after dinner. You can get a quite surprising amount of 'meat' into a five-minute speech—and by the same token you can make a ten-minute speech sound as though it has gone on for hours. I am occasionally asked for a speech lasting fifteen minutes in which to propose the toast to the Master. I always feel that such requests must come from brethren who have no idea how long a quarter of an hour can seem when the speaker is not an expert.

It can be dangerous to put the name of a person who is present into a joke. Everyone hasn't the same sense of humour, and while prepared to laugh at someone else's misfortune they may not find anything particularly funny in their own. Of course you can use a true anecdote about well-known people, but it does not make a story any funnier to laugh while telling it. And although suitable funny stories may help from the entertainment angle, it is as well to bear in mind that telling jokes isn't making a speech. If you want to employ dialect you must do it convincingly: otherwise it is dangerous. And I cannot insist too often that you should always speak sufficiently loudly to be clearly audible.

The examples which follow are intended to provide some essential material to enable you, having read this book, to put together speeches which will cover the requisite points while allowing you to put over your own personality. This latter really is important, for other masons besides you will have read the book! For the same reason it is inadvisable to employ (as some writers have suggested) a paraphrase of an article in the press.

Here, then, are some ideas for the toast to the visiting brethren or our guests. This one is designed to be given after an installation ceremony:

It is my pleasant duty to welcome all our guests. They come from far and wide. Some bring with them the good wishes of their respective lodges: others bring the determination to spend an enjoyable evening at the behest of those of our own brethren who are their hosts. As to the first, we are grateful for their good wishes which are heartily reciprocated. As to the second, we hope that in respect of enjoyment no brother has been disappointed.

I think it was Winston Churchill who said he liked short words and old words. I understand he also liked short speeches, but not old ones. His opinion was that half the world was composed of people who have something to say—and *can't*: and the other half was made up of people with *nothing* to say—who kept on saying it! Believe me, I have been keenly looking forward to proposing this toast—not because I have anything highly original to say, but because it gives me the opportunity to express the fraternal regard in which I, in common with all the brethren of the ... Lodge, hold our masonic brethren from other Lodges and Provinces.

So as each installation ceremony comes round we feel a renewal of warmth towards the brethren who, by their presence, honour our ceremony and our board. There is an old masonic song in which these words occur: 'We are met upon the Level and we part upon the Square.' As the Extended Working puts it: 'We are all sprung from the same stock, partakers of the same nature, and sharers in the same hope.' It is thus that we all wish to regard our visiting brethren. Brethren of the ... Lodge, I give you the toast: Our Visiting Brethren.

This also is suggested for delivery after an installation:

It has been said that men who, in the ordinary course, have not much in common can eat and drink together in perfect harmony, and rise from the table in a positive *glow* of brotherly love. How much more so, then, when we *start* as brothers! It affords me great pleasure this evening to welcome our visitors as true friends: and what joy there is in finding that a brother who, at the beginning of the evening, was a stranger, has, by the end of it, become a firm friend!

Our Lodge has been in existence for ... years, and as each succeeding installation comes round, the warmth with which we regard our visiting brethren becomes the greater. The Square, we learn, should be the guide of all our actions. Surely one of the most important of these is the encouragement of true brotherhood. And how easy and enjoyable this is on occasions such as installation nights! We wish all possible good for our visiting brethren. We trust that they have found the work in Lodge interesting, and the after-proceedings to their entire satisfaction. We are delighted to have them with us, and we hope they will all come again.

Brethren, I call upon you to be upstanding to drink a cordial toast to our Visiting Brethren.

This might be used by a brother (not the Master) who has been called on for the first time to propose the toast to the visiting brethren:

My greatest distinction in my ... years in Masonry has been my success in avoiding speaking at the festive board. Our visiting brethren will understand from this, either that this evening is a very important occasion, or else that the Master has been reduced to 'scraping the barrel!' Whatever may be your feelings on the subject, brethren, I assure you that there has been no barrel-scraping going on. Indeed, I rise with genuine sensations of pleasure and gratification to propose the toast to our visiting brethren.

I apologise to them at once for my shortcomings as a speaker, and I would claim that the one certainty about it all is my sincerity. It was either a gynaecologist or a midwife who defined a speech as a perfect *conception* followed by an easy *delivery*. As to the conception there can be no question of the ready welcome which every single one of us desires to extend to our guests. As to the delivery, I can only express the hope that in Lodge and at the after-proceedings we have satisfactorily delivered the goods.

I realise that one of the happiest points about proposing the toast to the visiting brethren is that many are already one's own friends. We owe you much, brother visitors, for playing your part in making our Lodge Meeting and this meal such a happy occasion.

I would suggest the following as the basis for the toast to the visiting brethren on a routine lodge occasion:

Although it is my pleasant duty to propose a toast to the *health* of our guests, I should like to assure them that, however much we may be concerned with their bodily fitness, the matter we regard as of even more importance is their *happiness*. It is well known that the only way to remain healthy is to eat what you don't want, drink what you don't like, and do what you'd rather not! Happiness, on the other hand, requires for its fulfilment that you should have someone to share it with. How happy we are, therefore, in Freemasonry, in possessing so many brethren with whom we are able to share our enjoyment! And how fortunate we are this evening in having with us such delightful guests!

We trust that the ceremony in Lodge was performed to our visitor's satisfaction, and we would assure them that any slight departures there may have been from the ritual with which they are familiar are to be put down to the immemorial custom of our lodge. We hope also that our board has come up to standard. Our visitors should disregard the idea that over-much indulgence in masonic dinners shortens the breath. Anyway, who on earth wants *long* breath? It's all very well to say an apple a day keeps the doctor away. One of my doctor friends says that a far more effective way of keeping the doctor away is to indulge in a diet of onions!

Brother visitors, having thus demonstrated our concern for your health and happiness, I shall call upon the brethren to rise and to drink the most fraternal of toasts to OUR GUESTS.

CHAPTER NINE

Replying for the Visitors

You can be certain that the task of replying for the guests or visitors will descend upon you without warning. For that reason, every Mason when visiting a lodge would be well advised to go equipped with some ideas as to what he will say. Anyone who has tried to gather material from the speech made by the proposer of the toast will be aware of the feeling of despair which follows the discovery that he has scribbled nothing in the least helpful on the back of the summons he has hopefully kept before him. He will also have experienced the sinking feeling which I have mentioned previously, when the Director of Ceremonies taps him on the shoulder with the request that he will reply for the visitors—thereby condemning him to spend the rest of the meal, not in happy conversation with his neighbours, but in puzzled searching for something to say.

All this can be avoided by the simple precaution of putting the outlines of a speech together, condensing them (if you like) to intelligible notes capable of emendation to accord with the occasion, and carrying them around in your pocket until they may be required. Once used, it would be wise to discard those notes and to write fresh ones; for at your next performance you may well be in the presence of brethren who heard your last effort. Wasn't it Bernard Shaw who said: 'You know very well that after a certain age a man has only one speech?' And the great Dr Samuel Johnson wrote: 'There may be other reasons for a man's not speaking in public than want of resolution: he may have nothing to say.' George Eliot wrote: 'Blessed is the man who having nothing to say, abstains from giving us wordy evidence of the fact.'

The brother replying for the visitors is expected to have something to say, although what he says ought not, in my opinion, to be necessarily either profound or educational. I have listened to after-dinner speeches from lodge visitors which I am sure must have cost them (or whoever wrote them) much time in research, and which, it has to be confessed, were quite unsuitable. References to the supposed antiquity of the Craft, and still less the recitation of obscure verse, has in my opinion no valid place in after-dinner speaking. Learned papers may be very acceptable in lodge, but not in the less serious atmosphere of the dinner table.

I set out below some suggestions in not too serious a vein for responses to the toast to the visitors:

In such a *distinguished* company as the present, you might well ask why so *undistinguished* a brother as I am should be called upon to reply to the toast. Let me express at once, Worshipful Master, the appreciation of your visitors of the kindly sentiments expressed by Brother ... in proposing our health. We are in no way surprised at the emotions which Brother ... has so tellingly voiced; for those of us who have visited your lodge in the past have invariably left with sincere gratitude for the fraternal regard of which you have contrived to leave us in no doubt.

In the matter of drinking our health I must say at once that already we all feel the better for it! As to your work in Lodge, Worshipful Master, I hope you will allow me to say in all humility that I consider the ceremony to have been carried out in accordance with the best tradition of your lodge by all concerned. And I would add that I should be very surprised if this view was not shared by those of your visitors who can boast longer experience and greater discernment than I have. So being met upon the Level we shall part upon the Square;

and in doing so we shall carry with us happy memories of an enjoyable evening.

Here is another suggestion:

I feel that it cannot be repeated too often that one of the most enjoyable aspects of Freemasonry is the pleasure to be obtained by visiting other lodges. We see each other at work as well as at play, and we are welcomed with a cordiality which has been well exemplified by Brother ... in proposing our health. In your hearty endorsement of the toast, brethren of the ... Lodge, you have demonstrated the spirit which, as we all know, exists between all Freemasons. As the Extended Working has it, we are indeed 'partakers of the same nature and sharers in the same hope.'

We are all conscious of the amount of solid work which goes into the preparation and successful carrying out of every masonic ceremony—the careful memorising and study in rehearsal and Lodge of Instruction—and even the odd feeling of anxiety. Then, if we are honest, comes that feeling of relief that it is all over. After all that we are but human in finding a little praise to be welcome. This being so, Worshipful Master, I should like to offer on behalf of all your visitors our sincere congratulations. There is an old Chinese proverb to the effect that if you bow at all, you should *bow low*. Your visitors will all join in bowing low in the confident hope that, having done so, we shall be invited again!

After an installation the number of visitors at dinner may well exceed the number of brethren of the lodge, and it is customary, and certainly desirable, that the responder should have been previously warned. Something like this may be considered suitable:

If I have understood him aright, Brother ..., in toasting those of us who are your visitors, has implied that our presence has given you pleasure. It is always gratifying to give pleasure—especially when you can do it at so little cost! Seriously, Worshipful Master and brethren, we are very happy to be here and to have had the honour of being present at the ceremony in Lodge. To this you have added the warmest of entertainment at your festive board.

On this very special occasion, Worshipful Master, your visitors would like to congratulate you most heartily on your elevation to the Chair of your Lodge. We should also like to congratulate the brethren of your Lodge on having acquired a Master of such outstanding qualities as yourself. We know, of course, of the long line of distinguished masters who have preceded you; and we are quite certain that you, as the ...th in that line, will do it honour.

As Master you will get a lot of pleasure out of attending other lodges over the coming year as the ambassador of your lodge, and some of us will be meeting you again in that connection.

Cheerfulness, they say, is the main ingredient of health, and the test of a good host is the enjoyment of his guests. Your Lodge has done us proud. You have not only entertained us most kindly with every mark of brotherhood, but you have even thanked us for coming. I can think of only one sentiment to add: please ask us again next year.

Sometimes after an installation there is, in addition to the toast to the visitors, a specific toast to the Masters in the Province. The response will, of course, be made by one of those masters, and might go as follows:

It gives me much pleasure to respond to the toast of the visiting masters. The great Dr Samuel Johnson wrote that *just* praise is only a debt, but *flattery* is a present. I shall regard Brother ...'s proposal of the toast as a welcome present, and thank him for it accordingly. I do not propose to flatter in return, however tempted I may be to do so. Instead I should like to express on behalf of the ruling masters our appreciation and approval of the sincerity, dignity and decorum with which your ceremony in Lodge was performed. We should like to offer sincere commendation to the installing master and his team of officers; and above all we should like to congratulate Worshipful Brother ... on becoming Master and consequently joining the select body whom I represent. We all hope that he will enjoy his year in the Chair, and that he will leave it at the end of his term with the feeling of having done well.

Having been well and truly installed, he has in the course of the ceremony been reminded to charge the brethren to practise out of the Lodge those duties they have been taught in it. As a ruling master I can assure him that he will obtain pleasure and satisfaction from his office, and I welcome him wholeheartedly to our ranks. We shall certainly meet again while visiting other lodges. We all anticipate such visits with pleasure, for we have the opportunity of coming up with brethren whom we seldom see elsewhere.

You, Worshipful Master, will from time to time be called upon (as I have) to reply to the toast of the visiting masters, and your neighbour may well remind you that you are having to sing for your supper. If that is what *I* am supposed to be doing, let me assure you that *your supper* is worth a great deal more than *my* feeble efforts to sing for it! So let me repeat, Worshipful Master, on behalf of all your future colleagues among the ruling masters, a hearty welcome accompanied by every good wish.

As I have said, the reply for the visitors need not be too frivolous, but should be lighthearted. Something like this perhaps:

There was a shipwrecked sailor who was cast ashore on a desert island with nothing more than the clothes he was wearing. Searching in his soaking pockets he came across a newspaper featuring one of the popular horoscopes. He looked for his own sign which read: 'You are going on a long journey. Do not enter on any financial dealings. This week you will have difficulty in making friends.' You will, I am sure, agree that in Masonry we have no difficulty in making friends, and that the most enjoyable way of meeting them lies in accepting invitations to visit other lodges. Not only do we see work as well done as yours, but we are also encouraged to do our best to emulate it.

The way in which you have entertained us at dinner has been beyond praise. You may have heard of Bernard Shaw's advice to the effect that you *should not* do unto others as you would wish that they should do to you: their tastes may not be the same as yours. This could well be true—but not this evening. Your tastes and ours have corresponded admirably. I feel that visits to other lodges do much to enable us (as the ritual puts it) to 'distinguish and appreciate the connection of our whole system.' Certainly such visits add to the fraternal enjoyment of all of us. This being so, your visitors all wish you well, and thank you for your generous entertainment.

CHAPTER TEN

The toast to Grand Lodge

More often than not this toast is given formally, but there may be an occasion on which something more is required. In that case it is essential that the speech should be prepared with more than ordinary care. Obviously the honour of being called upon to propose the toast must come first, and this could be followed by:

All honours bring with them certain obligations, the obligation in this case being to find something worthy to be said. If, from their seats in the Grand Lodge Above, those worthy brethren who met together on St John Baptist's Day in the year 1717 could see the outcome of their labours, what would their thoughts be?

The lodges that met at the Goose and Gridiron Alehouse in St Paul's Churchyard, at the Crown Ale-house in Parker's Lane, at the Apple-Tree Tavern in Charles Street, and at the Rummer and Grapes Tavern in Channel Row, decided, as a means of cementing a centre of Union and Harmony, to elect a Grand Master. Accordingly Anthony Sayers was (in the words of the minutes) forthwith invested and duly congratulated by the Assembly who paid him homage. Many changes have taken place over the years, and one of the most notable has been the very real interest which Royalty has taken in the Craft.

It is now our good fortune to have as our Grand Master Most Worshipful Brother His Royal Highness the Duke of Kent, whose enthusiasm for the Craft is evident to all of us. His predecessor of nearly 200 years ago, King William IV, was less well informed. When a deputation of influential Freemasons waited on him in expectation of a ceremonious audience, he is reported to have told them: 'Gentlemen, if my love for you equalled my ignorance of everything concerning you, it would be boundless.'

We are taught that it is the hope of reward that sweetens labour, and only very few of us can (in the nature of things) be rewarded with Grand Lodge Rank. Yet the *possibility* is there; and with it there is the constant encouragement to continue in well-doing. In this we can take to heart the oft-repeated truth that while some must govern, others must learn, submit and obey. So, brethren, I call upon you to be upstanding to drink the most cordial of toasts to Grand Lodge.

The reply generally comes from the most senior officer of Grand Lodge who happens to be present, but there is no rule about this. Indeed, his colleagues might prefer that the most recent addition to their ranks should reply. The response ought to be short, and consist mainly of thanks. If the preceding ceremony has been in installation, the new Master will be congratulated and wished well. If there has been an initiation the new-made brother will be welcomed into the Craft and reminded that in due course Grand Lodge will signify their approval by issuing him with a certificate to that effect.

Similarly, a Fellow Craft will be encouraged in the progress he has made, and a Master Mason will likewise be congratulated on having qualified for his master's apron. He will probably also be reminded that it is expected of him that he will in due course consider membership of the Royal Arch Chapter. I think that an Officer of Grand Lodge whose speech will come early in the list should try not to trespass on the territory of subsequent speakers, and this does limit to some extent what he can say. I would emphasise what I shall repeat from time to time, that you should never say that you don't know what your duties are. This statement removes at one fell swoop all the dignity from your office.

CHAPTER ELEVEN

The toast to Provincial Grand Lodge

It is customary for the Provincial Grand Master or one of his deputies to be present at installations. On such occasions the usual formal proposition of the toast to Provincial Grand Lodge is best replaced with something more telling from the Master. The expression of appreciation of what the Provincial Grand Master does for his Province is very right and proper, but it is unlikely that fulsome flattery will go down very well with most PGM's, the majority of whom do their utmost to be on the friendliest of terms with every brother they meet.

When the Provincial Grand Master or his deputy is present, the toast is to 'The Provincial (or Assistant) Grand Master, Right Worshipful Brother ... and the brethren of Provincial Grand Lodge.' If the PGM has sent one of his Wardens to represent him, the toast could be to 'The Representative of the Provincial Grand Master, Worshipful Brother ..., Provincial Junior Grand Warden, and the brethren of Provincial Grand Lodge.' Occasionally, as when a brother in the Lodge has received his Provincial Collar, it is felt to be appropriate to say a few words in toasting Provincial Grand Lodge, so that the new Provincial officer may have the opportunity to reply. Most lodges can boast a fairly high proportion of officers of Provincial Grand Lodge among their members, for most Past Masters are eventually elevated to Provincial Rank, as occasionally do especially meritorious brethren who have not attained the Chair. After a routine meeting the proposer of the toast

could be an officer or ordinary member of the Lodge, and
if the PGM has already been toasted, the toast becomes
one to Provincial Grand Lodge as an institution. Provincial
Grand Lodge officers who are members of the Lodge can
with advantage come in for comment, for they are those
who have done their stint on the floor of the Lodge and in
the Chair, and have been rewarded with the privilege of
wearing the darker blue.

Here, then are some ideas, the first one being for an
occasion when the Provincial Grand Master is present:

I regard it as an honour and a privilege to propose the
toast to our Provincial Grand Master, Right Worshipful
Brother.... In the course of his journeyings round the
Province the Provincial Grand Master must have heard
this toast given on countless occasions; and I expect that
at the drop of a hat he could recite the sentiments expressed therein. I would, however, venture to suggest
that on no occasion has the toast been given with
greater sincerity than the present. Nor have his virtues
been extolled with more genuine appreciation.

There is considerable advantage to all the brethren in
actually *knowing* their Provincial Grand Master, and in
the case of such a friendly ruler as ours this is easily
achieved. If I were going to preach a sermon about our
Provincial Grand Master I should take as my text two
passages which are not in the Volume of the Sacred
Law. The first is: 'A friend is a person with whom we
can always be sincere, and before whom we can think
aloud.' The other (from Samuel Johnson) is: 'A man, sir,
should keep his friendships in constant repair.' Wherever
our Provincial Grand Master may be, he is always the
first to extend his hand to greet you. Some brethren are
never quite sure what is expected of them in his presence, and these he invariably makes to feel at ease. It is
said that if you would have a friend you should *be* one.
This is what Masonry is all about. Promotion of our
brethren in Lodge to the ranks of Provincial Grand Lodge

in no way alters their position in regard to their brethren. They wear more glorious regalia, and we are proud of the progress they have made: and this evening we toast them in company with their ruler and ours. Brethren, I call upon you to be upstanding to drink the most loyal and friendly of toasts to our Provincial Grand Master, Right Worshipful Brother ..., and the officers of Provincial Grand Lodge.

This might be considered suitable when the Provincial Grand Master has sent his deputy or assistant:

I am privileged to propose the toast to Very Worshipful Brother ..., the Deputy Provincial Grand Master, and the officers of Provincial Grand Lodge, present and past. We hope that Very Worshipful Brother ... is feeling as much at home at our board as he did, to our great appreciation, in another place. An important part of the duty of the Deputy Provincial Grand Master is to ensure the maintenance of an acceptable standard of work throughout the Province. This can sometimes call for the exercise of a degree of *tact*—a quality which (if I may say so) is not lacking in our rulers in Provincial Grand Lodge. You may have heard it said that some people have *tact*, while others tell the truth! Dare I suggest that our rulers employ both?

Brethren of the Lodge who have been elevated to Provincial Grand Lodge will be the first to acknowledge that promotion to their ranks comes in due time to all who have earned it; and we are genuinely proud of the number of Provincial officers in this Lodge. We are grateful for the presence of the Deputy Provincial Grand Master, and in coupling his name with the toast I call upon you, brethren, to drink the most cordial of toasts to Provincial Grand Lodge.

On most routine occasions there is no-one specifically representing the Province, and in such cases the following might be given:

To propose the toast to Provincial Grand Lodge is always a pleasing experience to the proposer, even if his listeners may hold a different opinion. The proposer is not infrequently casting envious eyes on the dark blue collars in the Lodge, and calculating the date on which he himself would be well advised to start saving up for one! It is obvious to all of us of lesser rank that in the quite small Provincial team which is appointed each year there is room for only a tiny proportion of those worthy Past Masters whom the Provincial Grand Master would like to honour. Consequently the number of officers who actually *work* at their respective offices is very small compared with those who receive Past Rank.

Whether holding active or past rank, however, they are all selected from among those worthy masons who have served their lodges diligently and faithfully, and we offer them our fraternal and respectful affection. We acknowledge the good they do for the Craft—often in ways not known to the rest of us—and we applaud with enthusiasm the decision of the Provincial Grand Master whenever he elevates one of our brethren.

A suitable reply must, of course, be made to the toast to Provincial Grand Lodge. If this reply is to be made by an Assistant Provincial Grand Master, or by a brother who is present as the representative of the PGM, he may well have something to convey from the Province. This he will proceed to do after disposing of the customary courtesies. Such matters as the consecrating of a new lodge, or support for the Charities, or approaching centenary meetings can with advantage come into this response—even if reference has already been made to them in Lodge. Sometimes the matter of new entrants to the Craft can be raised from the standpoint of Provincial Grand Lodge. Some lodges have a waiting list of would-be initiates while others have difficulty in producing one a year. Why is this? Are we too secretive? Is there any reason why our best friends, or, come to that, the world at large, should *not* know that Freemasonry is a peculiar system of morality, veiled in allegory and illustrated by symbols?

As masons we do not claim to be any less fallible than the next man: but we do have an *ideal* before us. This is the sort of thing which might stimulate brethren to look around among their best-known friends who might (being reasonably instructed) be interested in joining us.

CHAPTER TWELVE

Some other toasts

The Installing Master, Past Masters and Officers of the Lodge
Many lodges give this toast just once a year after the installation ceremony. It is one of those toasts which seems to have become the prerogative of the Master, and it is not easy to see who else in Lodge could with propriety propose it, unless it be a senior brother who has never aspired to office. Most lodges have one or two such brethren, and frequently they are the salt of the earth. Most of them jib at making speeches, but if one can be got on to his feet for this toast the result might well be unusually acceptable. Something like this might do:

   With deep humility I rise from the ranks of the lowly to add my quota of praise for the work of the Installing Master, the Past Masters and the officers of the Lodge. Yet you may perhaps agree that my position calls for the exercise of a certain degree of tact. For consider this: to comment on the work of an Immediate Past Master might be considered in some quarters to be presumptuous when coming from the lips of a brother who is unlikely to get within miles of such an office. Similarly, for me to hold forth on the merits of a long line of distinguished Past Masters, and to dilate upon their meritorious service, would be to take for granted a degree of historical knowledge which it grieves me to have to confess that I do not possess.

   As to the officers, from my cosy corner in the lodge I can but marvel at the reliability of their memories. I watch their steady progress from the office of steward to the Chair, and when any one of them undertakes to be responsible for the explanation of the second tracing board I sit back comfortably and say to myself: 'I'd rather it was him than me!'

Worshipful Master and brethren, we are all proud, and I think justifiably so, of all those among us who carry out with such care and dignity the ceremonies of the Lodge. You, Worshipful Master, cannot have been other than deeply impressed this evening by the care and diligence with which Worshipful Brother ... installed you in the Chair. Our Past Masters provided in the ceremony examples of the manner in which they are, each and every one, ready and willing to be taken off the shelf to be given some work to do. When we come to consider the officers I feel that we of this Lodge have been especially fortunate in the quality of our officers. It is a matter of upbringing, of course, and of careful drilling by the Preceptor of the Lodge of Instruction, and by the Director of Ceremonies in Lodge.

So, as I have said, from the ranks of the lowly I am bold enough to call upon the brethren, both high and low, to toast with enthusiasm the Installing Master, the Past Masters and the officers of the Lodge.

If the Master is to propose the toast he will proceed on a different tack. Since he has just been installed, he will naturally wish to mention how impressed he was with the whole ceremony, and he will doubtless thank the Immediate Past Master who performed it. As to the Past Masters, he could congratulate the Immediate Past Master on joining their number after a successful year in the Chair. The officers will have been his own choice, and he will declare his confidence in their ability in their new offices, and his determination, with their enthusiastic assistance, to make his year a memorable one.

The Immediate Past Master

At the dinner following his installation the newly-installed Master may wish to single out his Immediate Past Master for a special toast. As the Immediate Past Master, in his capacity of Master throughout the preceding year, has been toasted with regularity after each meeting, it would be advantageous if something fresh could be found to say about him on this occasion. It is usual to present the Immediate Past Master in Lodge with his collar and jewel, and although some appropriate remarks will have been made at the presentation, these could be amplified and enlarged upon when proposing his health.

There are several fanciful explanations of the symbolical significance of the jewel and of the right-angled triangle, none of which (in my opinion) is likely to impress the recipient. It is far better to offer the collar as a badge of rank, and the jewel as a happy memento from his brethren of a memorable year of office. Presumably the Immediate Past Master will have done the installing ceremony, and he should therefore be accorded his due measure of praise on this account.

Opportunity might be taken to refer to any event of importance to the Lodge during the Immediate Past Master's mastership, such anniversaries, banner dedications, or any notable visitation, for there will be no further opportunity. Finally, attention might well be drawn to whatever may be the Immediate Past Master's principal relaxation—golf, philately, football, model railways, music, painting, do-it-yourself (he must have something)—and the hope can be expressed that, with less demands on his time by the Lodge, he will now have more leisure to devote to these important pursuits. I have even heard an Immediate Past Master congratulated on at last being free to give a proper attention to his daily work before his firm goes bankrupt!

The Installing Master, for one reason or another, may not be the retiring Master of the Lodge. In this case the new

Master may well wish to toast him separately. The Master will wish to thank him on behalf of all the brethren for stepping in to take the place of Worshipful Brother ... whose sudden illness prevented him from undertaking the duty. Whatever may be the reason, some graceful reference ought to be made to it, even if it should be the rather flimsy one of pressure of work. After all, the Master has had twelve months in which to learn the ritual: but here it should be said that if a master finds he really cannot memorise the work sufficiently to conduct the ceremony reasonably well, he should not hesitate to hand the job over to someone who can. One has very occasionally been the embarrassed witness of a master struggling ineffectually through an installation ceremony which he should never have tackled at all. The ceremony can be a moving experience if carried through properly by a master who has taken the trouble to learn and rehearse the ritual; but frequent prompting, or reference to book or notes, can destroy more than half its significance. 'It will be all right on the night' expresses an optimism which is seldom justified by results. So—if you feel that you cannot yourself do the job at least adequately, it is far better, despite the urgings of your brethren, to get a skilled Past Master to deputise for you. Remember that most lodges have a row of Past Masters all itching to be given some work to do; and among them there is sure to be one at least who will thank you for providing him with the opportunity to shine as once he shone before.

In such circumstances it would be a gracious act if the newly-installed Master were to give his Immediate Past Master the opportunity to propose the health of the Installing Master. In doing this there is no need to exaggerate the self-abasement. You had a good reason for finding yourself unable to do the ceremony up to the standard to which the Lodge had become accustomed, and you therefore called upon your old friend and brother, Brother ..., who, with characteristic helpfulness and alacrity, under-

took the task with the excellent result which has been
witnessed by all.

I do not feel that there is need to expatiate further, and
in his reply the Installing Master will probably thank you
for inviting him to perform a ceremony in which he enjoyed
every moment. He will finish by adding his felicitations to
those of all the brethren in wishing the Master a happy
year of office.

Here is an example of a short and pithy reply made by
the Immediate Past Master:

In thanking you, Worshipful Master, for your kind words,
and you, brethren, for the warmth of your endorsement
of them, let me make a confession. I feel I must say that,
greatly as I have enjoyed my year in the Chair, I cannot
now repress a certain feeling of (shall we say) relief that
it is over. With that relief, however, comes the best of all
possible good wishes for a happy and useful year for
you, Worshipful Master. As to your officers, each one
newly appointed to a more senior office (except for the
secretary who, like Tennyson's brook, goes on forever)
I have no doubt that, under your guidance, they will
carry out their duties with their customary fervency and
zeal. (Any outstanding memory of the year might be re-
called here.) Let me assure you, Worshipful Master and
brethren, that wherever my future situation in the Lodge
may be, I shall ever remain entirely at your service.

The Master Elect

At the dinner following the ceremony at which he has been
elected, it is a pleasing custom to toast the Master Elect.
This could be done in the following words:

The office of Master is the highest honour which the
Lodge has it in its power to confer. It is also an indication
of the very real regard in which you are held, Brother
..., by each and every brother in the Lodge. This will be
brought home to you in the course of the ceremony of
your installation, but for the moment it will be sufficient

to say that your brethren have the most complete confidence in your ability to uphold the high standards which have always been associated with our Lodge. Those of us who have occupied the Chair are well aware of the responsibilities attaching to the office, and we should like to assure you of our co-operation and assistance at all times. Indeed we shall feel delighted if one or other of us might occasionally be taken off the shelf, dusted and given a little work to do. Meanwhile, Master Elect, please accept our congratulations and best wishes. Brethren, I give you the toast: Brother ..., our Master Elect.

To this the Master Elect might care to reply as follows:
First I must return thanks for the kindly remarks which have been made about me, and for the warmth of their reception. It has been pointed out to all my predecessors in the Chair that every candidate for the office of Master ought to be of good report, true and trusty, and held in high estimation among his brethren and fellows. To be so described gives me a feeling of humility. In the Volume of the Sacred Law it is laid down: 'He that would be chief among you, let him be your servant.' I shall try to bear that in mind, brethren, and I promise you that I shall do my duty zealously and faithfully: and I hope that in twelve months' time I shall be able to hand over in the consciousness that I have done my best. Thank you, brethren.

Depending upon circumstances, the Master Elect might in his reply seize on the offer of assistance and thank the Past Masters accordingly, assuring them that he will be only too pleased to give them some work to do. On the other hand, he may have different ideas. He might also wish to thank any individual brother who has helped him on his way: sometimes his proposer and seconder come into this category. Finally he can assure the brethren

that he looks forward to his installation with eager
expectancy.

The Master in the Chair

It happens from time to time that the Chair has to be taken,
for one reason or another, by a deputy who is usually the
Immediate Past Master. He is toasted at the after-proceedings and then has to say a few words in reply. There is no
reason why he should not say that, while he has been
pleased to take the Master's place on a temporary basis, he
would not wish to conceal from the brethren that he will
be as glad as they will to see the Master back again. I do
not think that this is the right occasion for an excessive
display of modesty, nor for any apology for not doing the
work as well as the Master would. After all, the Master in
the Chair may have taken the job on at short notice, and
in such cases the brethren are always ready and anxious to
be understanding. If the Master's absence is due to illness,
his progress will doubtless have been reported on in
Lodge, but the wish can still be expressed for his early
recovery. Reference might also be made to any other
gap-filler who should be suitably thanked.

The Officers

Occasionally the Master may wish to single out his officers
for a toast, separating them from the more usual toast
which includes the Past Masters. This, I feel, is very much
a personal appreciation of each officer as a brother. The
Master might care to proceed in this manner:

> The Lodge is singularly blessed with a treasurer whom
> *we* treasure, and a secretary who treasures *us*: a Director
> of Ceremonies endowed with the required virtues of
> confidence coupled with dignity: and Wardens who are
> ever conscious of the part they play in assisting me in
> the ruling and governing of the Lodge. As for the
> Deacons, you will all know that their attention to their
> candidates is all that could be desired.

When you come to think of it, a candidate at his initiation has, in his own mind, only one friend in the world—the Junior Deacon. And how important it is, brethren, that the Junior Deacon should be able to convey through the ritual a feeling of warmth and friendliness to his new-made brother! This, I feel, has always been the object of a succession of good Junior Deacons. I would assure our Assistant Secretary that he could not have a more efficient mentor than our secretary, ther.... This goes also for our Assistant Director of Ceremonies, whose tutor combines tact with kindness. Brother.... This goes also for our Assistant Director of Ceremonies, whose tutor combines tact with kindness. appears—and we all wish him success as he makes his way up the ladder.

Finally, brethren, I should like to urge a regular attendance at Lodge of Instruction. By this means you will attain confidence in your ability to undertake all the offices with pleasure to yourselves and satisfaction to your brethren.

The following will provide the basis for a reply:
On behalf of the officers of the Lodge, both commissioned and non-commissioned (if I may put it that way) I must thank you for the kindly sentiments expressed in toasting our health. Let me assure you, Worshipful Master, that you, as our employer, may be surprised to learn that we *enjoy* working for you. We are never tempted to hold union meetings during the working of the Lodge, and our Stewards regard themselves as the servants of the brethren rather than their leaders!

Our progress in masonry resembles our journey through adult life; so that from our relatively menial tasks as stewards we proceed by way of one of the most satisfying undertakings in masonry—that of piloting a candidate through his initiation ceremony—to doing most of our work sitting down, as wardens. Then eventually there comes the Chair. I should like to suggest that as each officer makes his way upwards, the learning and performance of the ritual results in his gaining something in moral and ethical stature—perhaps a little more wisdom, and maybe a touch of humility. Worshipful Master and brethren, thank you again for drinking the health of the officers of the Lodge. Thank you also for undertaking that last and greatest trial—having to listen to me!

The Master Mason

Every mason on the occasion of his Raising deserves a toast to himself at the after-proceedings, even if that toast is only formal. My own feeling is that at least a few words should be said, preferably by his proposer. If the proposer feels that he has had his say after the initiation, then the seconder might well be called upon. This speech provides an opportunity to tell the new Master Mason something of the history of the Craft, but I am well aware that many of the brethren (whose views I respect) consider that the Lodge and not the dinner table is the proper place for such instruction. This being so, the following might provide an idea for the toast to the new Master Mason:

As Brother ...'s proposer (seconder) it gives me much pleasure to propose his health on the occasion of his Raising. He is now in possession of the secrets of a master mason, and entitled to wear his own apron and gloves! He will understand that these articles of clothing symbolise the accoutrements worn by our predecessors, the operative masons of medieval times, in whose footsteps we tread. It is our firm belief that membership of a masonic lodge is a guarantee of good order; for its brethren, by the terms of their obligation, set a good example to the community. The Square and Compasses represent the positive and negative springs of conduct. A brother's activities are represented by the Square, and his restraints by the Compasses.

We all of us hope that Brother ... will enjoy many

happy years in Freemasonry, and I call upon you, brethren, to be upstanding to drink a cordial and fraternal toast to Brother....

The response will give the Master Mason an opportunity, which he will not have had since his initiation, of trying his wings as a speaker. Having dealt with thanking the proposer of the toast, he could proceed like this:

I am very conscious that I have in the course of the recent ceremony been given a title for which our operative forbears laboured for many years. Even an apprentice in their days served his master for seven years. Freemasonry has opened my eyes to many hitherto unknown facts, and I am proud to be associated with its system of morality.

As a very new mason I should like to mention that I have been impressed by the tenets of Brotherly Love, Relief and Truth. These, as I understand it, support the whole edifice of our institution. I regard it as a privilege to be addressed as 'Brother' and to address others in the same way. And since my apron is to be considered as the 'badge of innocence and the bond of friendship' I shall always wear it with pride and affection. And finally, I assure you that I shall do my best to be worthy of your fraternal regard.

London Grand Rank

This is the equivalent in London of Provincial Grand Rank, and all the sentiments set out under the heading of Provincial Grand Rank apply. It is customary to refer to the appointment to London Grand Rank as an indication, not only of the honour and regard in which the recipient is held, but also as expressing the hope of further service to the Craft. The toast is frequently combined with that of the Provincial officers under the heading of 'Officers of London and Provincial Grand Rank'.

Presentation of a Grand Lodge Certificate and Jewel
These two presentations are made in Lodge and do not
really call for further reference after dinner. Nevertheless, if
they are to be mentioned, the time might be suitable to
give the possessor of the certificate a few hints on visiting
strange lodges, and also on the method by which he will
have to prove himself if no brother can vouch for him. This,
of course, will have to be done with much discretion. The
warning against getting involved with unrecognised
quasi-masonic bodies cannot be given too early, for it is
the comparatively new mason who is most likely to be
caught up in these.

The recipient of the Jewel will have returned thanks in
Lodge, and, unless he is on his feet for a speech, is unlikely
to have anything further to say. He may wish to assure the
brethren that he will wear the representation of the Square
and Compasses above his heart, not only as a reminder of
the principles of morality and propriety, but also as a memento of a very happy year.

Consecration of a new lodge
The required speeches at the consecration dinner usually
consist of a toast to the founders of the lodge, and one to
the consecrating officers. Both are in the nature of thanks
for work well done; and the consecrating officers are
usually elected to honorary membership.

In replying to the toast to the founders it would be well
to mention the Mother Lodge and the assistance given by
its brethren. The response would probably be made by the
first Master who would express the hope that the new
lodge would add lustre to the town and province. He
would go on to acknowledge that the honour of the Craft
has been entrusted to the new lodge, and that that responsibility would always be in the forefront of the minds
of the brethren. The Master might conclude in these terms:

The world judges Freemasonry not by what is *best* in it,

but by what is *worst*. We, as a new lodge, shall do our best to uphold the dignity of the Craft both in the lodge and outside it. We shall resist any temptation to admit other than thoroughly worthy candidates who can be relied upon to respond to masonic teaching and principles. At the same time we shall bear in mind that we are no long-faced community, and that one of our objects is to be happy and to communicate happiness. We repeat our thanks to the Right Worshipful Provincial Grand Master and his team for bringing our lodge into being, and we promise that it will forever do them credit.

If the toast is made to the Lodge rather than to the first Master, the reply might be made in these terms:

It falls to me to respond to the toast to a Lodge which, until a few short hours ago, did not exist. The brothers will recall that in the course of the consecration the Right Worshipful Provincial Grand Master employed these words: 'To God and to His service we dedicate this Lodge.' So, brethren, let us ever bear in mind that, in carrying out our masonic duties, we stand on holy ground. The ceremony comes as a most useful means of reminding us all of certain aspects of the Craft which are otherwise not infrequently overlooked.

The scattering of corn as a symbol of plenty might well remind us of our obligation to the masonic charities, for Relief or Charity comes next after Brotherly Love in the three prime tenets of our profession.

The pouring of wine, symbolising joy and cheerfulness, reminds us of the reference in the ritual to that grand design of being happy and communicating happiness. Brethren, the act of communicating happiness may well be considered the more important of the two, especially since it is one of the virtues to be exercised outside the lodge.

Finally in these troublous times surely the pouring of oil as a sign of peace and unanimity cannot do other than encourage us in our efforts to calm the disturbances of an all too frequently unhappy and quarrelsome world. As an institution we are frequently criticised and derided by people who know nothing about us. The occasional book is produced by a non-mason, and supposed ceremonies appear on television. The best response is a dignified silence, for there is no denying that by some people we are regarded with suspicion—especially after exposures concerning a continental lodge of so-called masons who have no connection whatever with genuine Freemasonry. Brethren, as a new lodge, we shall do our best to make a daily advancement in masonic knowledge, and we rely upon the Great Architect to prosper our work.

The Lodge of Instruction
Not every lodge has its Lodge of Instruction. Some rely on rehearsals for preparing the work, and some, regrettably, do not even regularly rehearse. Whatever happens or does not happen in this respect is bound to show up in the standard achieved in the carrying out of the ceremonies in lodge. If the officers are to experience the pleasure which they ought to have in performing their duties well, it is essential that they should know the work thoroughly before they venture on to the floor in open lodge.

The most obvious usefulness of a Lodge of Instruction is that brethren can proceed through all the offices well before they are called upon to undertake them in lodge. The Lodge of Instruction is not a substitute for rehearsals: rather is it a pleasant and friendly preparation for them, and a means of gaining confidence. I had only been a mason for three years, and was sitting in lodge waiting for the opening, when the Director of Ceremonies came in from the anteroom and said: 'You were Junior Deacon in an initiation in Lodge of Instruction last week, weren't you?' I replied that I was. 'Fine!' said the Director of Ceremonies, 'The Junior Deacon hasn't arrived, so you can do his job to-night.' And I did: which is perhaps why I still feel, forty years on or more, that the Junior Deacon's part in an initiation is the most enjoyable in the whole ritual!

Under a good preceptor the membership of a Lodge of Instruction can provide at least as much enjoyment as teaching, for there is an air of informality about most of them, and some even come up once a year with their own Ladies' Night. The Lodge of Instruction is seldom toasted at the lodge after-proceedings, but if it is so toasted the proposer could voice the sentiments I have mentioned above. I will deal with the Lodge of Instruction's Ladies' Night under its own heading.

The Masonic Charities

Most lodges afford their Charity Steward an opportunity to make his annual appeal at the Installation dinner by calling for a toast to the Royal Masonic Institutions.

It is a sad fact that too many brethren regard their contributions to the Masonic Charities as some kind of additional benevolence which is quite separate from their lodge subscription. In fact the sum allocated to charity ought to be of at least equal significance. We talk glibly of Brotherly Love, Relief (that is Charity) and Truth, and tend to forget that, in the words of the Volume of the Sacred Law, 'the greatest of these is charity.' The Charity Steward is presumed to be well versed in his subject, and therefore able to advise the brethren once a year on how, as a lodge, they are doing. Some Provinces set a target for each lodge, thereby simplifying the job of an unenthusiastic Charity Steward who, having reached his target, is tempted to sit back and do no more about the brethren who are manifestly subscribing too little, or have ceased subscribing altogether. He should never have to beg, for charity is a duty which is incumbent on all of us. Charity Jewels are available for brethren who wish to wear them. Some, however, prefer not to advertise their subscriptions to the Charities. I hasten to add that this is my own purely personal view.

The Board of General Purposes feels that every member of the Craft should possess a copy of the booklet entitled *Information on Masonic Charities*. I subjoin some extracts:

0103. As a general summary, brethren have been encouraged, from the beginning of speculative Masonry, to give money or time for the relief of poverty or distress. The objects have not always been linked exclusively to Freemasonry, and more emphasis is now being given to non-Masonic charity.

0104. A general Charity was established soon after Grand Lodge was founded in 1717, and eventually became the Board of Benevolence. A school for the daughters of Freemasons was opened in 1788, and a charity for clothing and educating the sons of indigent brethren established in 1798. These institutions became the Royal Masonic Institution for Girls and the Royal Masonic Institution for Boys. Care for aged and sick brethren and their wives or widows by housing them or paying annuities started in 1842, and the Royal Masonic Benevolent Institution was formed in 1850. The forerunner of the Royal Masonic Hospital was founded in 1911, and the present building at Ravenscourt Park was opened in 1933. The chronological order of establishment of the Masonic Charities has been followed in this booklet, with the new combined Charities following the Charities from which they have emerged.

0105. As a result of the recommendations of a Committee set up by the MW The Grand Master to enquire into the future of the main Masonic Charities (the Bagnall Committee), which reported in 1973, the Masonic Charities have been or are being reorganised, so that:

    a. the Grand Charity, constitutionally independent of the Grand Lodge but having the same membership, has taken over the functions of the Board of Benevolence;

    b. the Masonic Trust for Girls and Boys will unite the

Royal Masonic Institution for Girls and the Royal Masonic Institution for Boys and

c. the Masonic Foundation for the Aged and the Sick is acting as a fund raising body on behalf of the Royal Masonic Benevolent Institution and the Royal Masonic Hospital.

0201. The Grand Charity exists . . . to relieve distressed Master Masons and their dependants, and provide funds for charitable work, mainly that of the Masonic Institutions, although money is also given to non-Masonic Charities.

0211. The relief of Petitioners will continue to be a most important and significant part of recurring expenditure.

0601. The Royal Masonic Benevolent Institution provides annuities for Freemasons under the English Constitution, their widows, spinster daughters and spinster sisters of sixty years of age, and over, or under this age if incapacitated, and runs Residential Homes in various parts of England and Wales.

0702. The Royal Masonic Hospital is an independent 263 bedded hospital for acute general medicine and surgery, primarily for Freemasons and their dependants, especially those who need but cannot afford the costs of private medicine, surgery and nursing. It is not a casualty hospital, but will admit patients in an emergency at any time. The Hospital has a training school for State Registered and State Enrolled Nurses.

0710. The Hospital's Samaritan Fund is separate from its general funds and exists to help the patients who cannot afford the Hospital's full fees, according to their circumstances.

CHAPTER THIRTEEN

Occasional speeches

Such matters as congratulations on promotion to Grand Rank or to Provincial or London Grand Rank, the restoration to health of a brother, or his death, would have been dealt with in Lodge, and would call for no specific reference (except in passing) at the after-proceedings.

CENTENARY MEETINGS do not, in the nature of things, come very often, and when they do they invariably merit the attendance of the team from Provincial Grand Lodge. Some brother (usually the secretary) gets the job of writing a history of the Lodge, and this is duly printed as a brochure. The labour of the Lodge is laid down by Provincial Grand Lodge who will instruct the Master, the Director of Ceremonies and the secretary in detail as to what is required of them.

The Lodge will doubtless in a hundred years have sponsored other lodges whose Masters will be present; and at the after-proceedings it may be considered appropriate to welcome the representatives of these 'daughters'. Some reference can be made to the fact that not many mothers live to be a hundred, and the ages of the daughters can come in for comment. The order of their birth might be worth mentioning, and it might not be out of place to suggest that 'mother' continues to keep a watchful eye on them.

A RE-JOINING BROTHER is sometimes called upon to speak after dinner. He may be toasted and will therefore have to reply. His response will be very much of a personal nature, depending on his reasons for leaving the Lodge — generally removal to a distance. The re-joining brother may well be getting on in years, in which case he can comment that he has reached the time in life which is best described as his *Anecdotage*, having survived (so many) years in the Craft. He may feel proud to look back and discover that amid all the changes and chances of life although the faces of the brethren may change, the ceremonies and the brotherhood remain exactly as they always were. Several references to age appear among the chapter of quotations, and the speaker may well be able to pin something on to one or other of these. Our brother should finish with his thanks to the Master and brethren for the welcome he has received on his return to the fold, following this with his best wishes for the future happiness and prosperity of all the brethren.

At the end of a LADIES' NIGHT the President sometimes likes to say a few words of farewell. The occasion for this would normally be after the singing of *Auld Lang Syne*, and would not entail anything in the nature of a speech. All that is required is the expression of the President's thanks to everyone for their presence, and the hope that they will each have a safe journey home. He will look forward to seeing the ladies again at the next Ladies' Night, and the brethren at the next Lodge Meeting.

DEATH OF A BROTHER. The Master may well wish to make reference to a brother's death which has occurred since the last lodge meeting. It is better to be sincere and simple rather than fulsome, and nothing is to be gained by attributing to the deceased brother masonic qualities which he did not possess. On the other hand, if he had been a regular attender and had achieved distinction as Master or in any other office, reference ought to be made to this. Something on these lines might be acceptable:

Brethren, the Lodge has suffered a sad loss in the pass-ing to the Grand Lodge Above of Brother .... It was good to see so many of his brethren who had gathered at his funeral to pay a last tribute of respect to departed merit. Initiated in ..., and Master in ..., our brother had always shown a notable love for Masonry and a sincere affection and regard for all his brethren. His worth had been acknowledged by Provincial Grand Lodge, and the Provincial Grand Master has sent a kind letter of condolence. Our most abiding memory of our brother may well be in connection with . . . . . ., when his truly masonic qualities were most in evidence. We offer to his wife and family our very sincere sympathy, and we assure them that we shall ever remember Brother ... with affection and pride. For to live in hearts we leave behind is not to die.

LONG SERVICE so seldom gets acknowledged that these few words may serve as a reminder:

Brethren, how often we take for granted the work of our long-serving brethren! They tend to assume the same significance as the furnishings: we don't especially notice them when they are in their accustomed position, but we immediately become aware when for any reason they are not there. Brother ... has served us all in exemplary fashion for ... years with a devotion which has earned him the love and respect of all of us. I want to assure him that we of the ... Lodge do *not* regard him as an article of furniture, and that we are more grateful than we can say for his devoted work in the Lodge.

It is not often that THE SECRETARY is made the subject of a toast. Even when he has intimated that he does not wish to be included in the list of officers for the forthcoming session it is not common practice for much to be said about it at the after-proceedings. If it does occur to the Master that references should be made to the secretary, something on these lines might be suitable:

Brethren, you will perhaps be surprised to know that our secretary, Brother ..., does not wish to be re-appointed. Masters come and Masters go, and the one solid rock to which the Lodge is fixed is more often than not the secretary. He is the brother to whom we all turn, Master and brethren alike, for guidance. How often have we heard him say, 'Yes, Worshipful Master: Just as you say, Worshipful Master: NO—I'm afraid you can't do that!' He is always the backbone of the Lodge and never the wishbone.

A BROTHER WHO HAS CONTRIBUTED A LECTURE will in the normal course have been thanked in Lodge, but should further acknowledgment be required, something like this might suit:

We are recommended in Lodge to make a daily advancement in masonic knowledge. Such a course of study would scarcely come within the ambit of most of us. Indeed, many only pick up their knowledge of the history of Freemasonry from the limited opportunities which arise to listen to speakers who have, as it were, done our homework for us. Brother ...'s discourse has without doubt opened doors for many of us, and may well have strengthened in us the love and respect we all hold for our brotherhood. For this, Brother ..., we are all much beholden to you, and we look forward with pleasure to hearing you again.

CHAPTER FOURTEEN

The Ladies' Night

This is the only function of the year which is enjoyed not only by the Mason but also by his wife and family. By the average Mason it is regarded as an opportunity to demonstrate to his wife the fact that on lodge evenings he is in the company of a highly respectable group of men. Most wives look forward eagerly to the annual Ladies' Night, since it enables their husbands to say a practical thank you for their wives' endurance of many solitary evenings.

Apart from this, however, there is about Masonic Ladies' Nights an unmistakable aura which is not to be found in other similar occasions. Possibly the fact that we are in the possession of certain secrets gives the affair some attraction for the ladies. I am told that in Victorian days the brethren used to appear at Ladies' Nights in their aprons and collars, but this practice together with any other 'outward and visible signs' has long been proscribed. Although there remain a few lodges which refer to the Worshipful Master by his masonic title at Ladies' Nights, the use of masonic titles is frowned upon by Grand Lodge in other than purely masonic contexts. The Master is to be referred to as Presiding Officer or President, and I am told that the ladies find this disappointing—especially the Master's lady!

It comes naturally enough to Masons in Lodge to address the Master and all the officers by their rank, but a little thought will show how inappropriate this is at a mixed gathering of ladies, Masons and non-Masons. I have heard ladies beginning the reply to their toast with 'Worshipful Master and Brethren', following this with references to

Brother Smith and Brother Jones. A helpful husband has probably put them up to this, but the usage is quite wrong. Although intended kindly, it tends to turn a serious institution into a bit of a joke. I can see no harm in calling upon 'Brother Smith, our Junior Warden' to propose the toast to the ladies, and in her reply the responder might be expected to have something to say about wardens. Similarly the Master's wife knows perfectly well that in the Lodge her husband is regarded as worshipful, and she could hardly be expected to refrain from having something to say about that in her reply.

Besides following the customary form of delicate flattery, the toast to the ladies provides an opportunity to make reference to any particular service which any lady or ladies have given to the lodge. If the responder is well known to the proposer he may be able to say something about her interests and pursuits. The principal point to be made is the pleasure and honour which is felt by all the members of the Lodge in having their ladies with them, coupled with the hope that they are enjoying themselves.

The tone of all the speeches at a Ladies' Night is altogether lighter and more 'off duty' than at lodge occasions. At the same time it must be borne in mind that, since ladies are present, even greater care than usual must be taken to see that nothing offensive is included. Male non-Masons will also be there, and to that extent the Craft will be on show.

Before proceeding to the provision of some specimen speeches I should like to reproduce the Menu and Toast List of a Ladies' Night at which I presided in 1950. Here an ingenious secretary had provided a few words extracted from the ritual after each item on menu and toast list. Although this does not accord with the recommendation that there should be no reference at a Ladies' Night to what goes on in Lodge, I feel that the amusement which this programme provided for the brethren was worth the puzzled enquiries of the 'uninstructed and popular world'.

The Master was so referred to in those days. At the heading was the Grace, which I reproduce for the sake of completeness, and also because it is sometimes incorrectly quoted. This and the quotations from the ritual were printed in italics.

GRACE

For these and all Thy mercies given,
We bless and praise Thy name, O Lord,
May we receive them with thanksgiving,
Ever trusting in Thy word.
To Thee alone be honour and glory,
Now and henceforth for evermore.
                              Amen.

MENU
'Which I recommend to your serious perusal.'

*   *

Hors D'oeuvres
'Mysteries of Nature and Science'

*   *

Roast Chicken
Roast and Creamed Potatoes: Green Peas and Vichy Carrots
'I need not here dilate upon its excellence.'

*   *

Fresh Fruit Salad and Ice Cream
'The reward that sweetens labour.'

*   *

Biscuits and Cheese
'Ancient no doubt it is.'

*   *

Coffee
'The last and greatest trial.'

*   *

TOAST LIST
'Regularly proposed and approved.'

*   *

His Majesty the King
'The allegiance due to the Sovereign of your native land.'

*   *

The Ladies
'The constant care of every Mason.'

*   *

The Worshipful Master
'I give it you in strong terms of recommendation.'

*   *   *

Here are some ideas for the toast to The Ladies:

My object in proposing this, the most important toast of the evening, is to express appreciation—deep appreciation—of our ladies. The dictionary defines APPRECIATION as 'to be fully sensible of all good qualities.' I sometimes wonder, brethren, if we are all fully sensible of the good qualities possessed by our ladies. It occurs to me sometimes, and this evening in particular, that we may not always be conscious of our ladies' self-sacrifice in surrendering the pleasure of our company to the call of our lodges: and this not only on lodge nights, but also for Lodge of Instruction, visiting and so on.

And let us look back upon the time when we were taking office, and our long-suffering wives had to endure long periods of absent-mindedness while we pored over our little book and then retired to the bathroom to see if we could recite what we hoped we had learned.

This Ladies' Night provides us with an opportunity to make some small amend for our neglect, and maybe to say a few of the flattering things which we too often omit on less glamorous occasions. So, ladies, it is our most sincere hope that you are enjoying yourselves, and that you will remember this as a happy off-shoot (if I may so describe it) of your husbands' Masonry.

We look forward to hearing ...'s response to this toast—not least because we regard her husband as one of the ornaments of our lodge. An ornament, as you know, is one of those objects which all ladies like to cherish and keep clean and bright! Here, then, is just one word of male advice to all the ladies: always remember that husbands are like wood fires. If left unattended they go out! Gentlemen, in asking you to couple the toast with the name of ..., I bid you rise and drink the most loving of toasts to the ladies.

Here is a toast from a slightly different angle:

In proposing the toast to the ladies I should not like you to think that my object is merely to court popularity. Neither is it to flatter—for I mean every word I say. As I look around the tables I am struck by the youth and beauty of the ladies, and, honestly, if I had been a teen-ager on the street watching them come in this evening, I should have been tempted to whistle—except that I *couldn't*, because my tongue was hanging out! It is my serious belief that women really are 'the better half'. What did that great poet, Robert Burns, have to say about it? He said of Nature that 'her 'prentice hand she tried on man, an' *then* she made the lassies.' In the Garden of Eden, Eve followed Adam, but when they were turned out it was Eve who went first. And woman, you will observe, has preceded man ever since.

Let me quote Burns again: 'The sweetest hours that e'er I spend are spent among the lassies.' Gentlemen and brethren, we spend, it is true, many happy hours *away* from the company of our ladies (notably on masonic occasions), but how much happier we are in their company on a night like this! We know that we can never adequately repay our ladies for all they do for us, but we hope they will take the will for the deed and look upon this evening as some small recompense.

I hope that ..., who is to respond to this toast, has been able to make some sense out of my ramblings; but even if she hasn't we look forward with happy expectancy to hearing her. Brethren, I give you the toast of long life, health and happiness to the ladies.

The response is quite often made by the President's wife who will probably be well known to the proposer of the toast. He will in that case refer to her by her Christian name, and may possibly care to look up its meaning and follow this by finding virtues for her beginning with each letter of her name. The name MARY, for example, is said to mean 'Wished for', and her virtues could be M for Merry, A for Attractive, R for Reasonable and Y for Youthful. With the help of the dictionary you may well be able to find more fitting qualities.

Sometimes the toast is entrusted to a fairly new member of the lodge, and the speaker can make something out of this in this way:

To be invited to propose the most important speech of the evening when you are as new to Masonry as I am, is to be taken either as a great honour to the speaker, or else as a willingness to run extreme risks on the part of the organiser. I do not propose to announce that I am no speechmaker, because that will become obvious as I go along: but I should like (if I could) to say something which is not unworthy of the gracious lady who is to respond. So I shall proclaim at once that woman is NOT man's equal: she is his SUPERIOR. What is more, she *looks* his superior; for as my enraptured gaze wanders around the tables I am struck by the fact that all the ladies look so much younger than their escorts.

Ladies, we hope that you approve of the men we get about with on our Masonic occasions. We should all like you to know how much we appreciate your readiness to relinquish the pleasure of our company on such evenings—and all without a word of reproach. Well, *almost* without a word, shall we say?

The response to this toast is to come from a lady who, I am quite certain, is a far better speaker than I am. I shall therefore call upon you to couple her name with the toast which I shall give you. Mr President and gentlemen, the toast is to the long life, health and happiness of THE LADIES.

Here is another slightly frivolous suggestion:

As each annual Ladies' Night comes round, has it ever struck you, gentlemen, that we men all look that little bit *older*, and our ladies look the same little bit *younger*? There is an old song which goes: 'A *man* is as old as he's feeling; a *woman's* as old as she looks.' Ladies, you have no idea how glad we are to have you with us on this happy Ladies' Night. You have provided us with the opportunity to make some small return to you for giving up our company on lodge nights with scarcely a word of reproach.

You seem to do everything so much better than we do. Some men seem to need two women in their life: a secretary to take things down, and a wife to pick things up! Somebody told me years ago that if your wife doesn't treat you *as she should*—you ought to be thankful! The same man, who obviously knew what he was talking about, suggested that a truly truthful woman is one who won't lie about anything—except her age, her weight, and her husband's salary! So, ladies, let me assure you on behalf of all the men that we admire you for your beauty, respect you for your intelligence, and love you for your virtue. This being so, I shall call upon all the gentlemen to be upstanding to drink the most loving of toasts to THE LADIES.

The reply to the toast to the ladies is most frequently made by the Master's lady. The shortest in my experience was that provided many years ago by my own wife who, shaking in every limb, rose and said: 'Mr Chairman, ladies and gentlemen, thank you very much.' Although this brought forth enthusiastic applause, it is not to be unreservedly recommended. Ladies in general are not normally lost for words, but to reply gracefully to a flattering speech from a reasonably skilled proposer is not given to everyone.

Many gain the ear of their audience at once by confessing to nervousness. Genuine nervousness often manifests itself by starting to speak before everyone is quiet. So yet again I would repeat my dictum: first obtain complete silence. Of one thing the lady speaker can be completely confident: she has the utter goodwill of all her audience who are anxious to applaud everything she says. And if and when they do applaud, the speaker will of course wait for them to finish before she continues.

A Ladies' Night is an occasion for jollity, and there is no reason why the Master's lady should not indulge in a little gentle leg-pulling at her husband's expense. She will probably have something to say about the proposer of the toast, and she will on behalf of all the ladies thank the members of the Lodge for providing so happy an evening. The ladies will probably each have received a present, and, unless it is ceremonially presented separately, the Master's lady will also have been given a personal gift and flowers, either or both. And she will remember (whatever she may have been told) that she must never refer to a member of the lodge as 'brother'.

She may possibly find a reference to her hobbies or those of her husband to be useful; for personal and domestic references in this friendly speech of thanks are always well received. Ladies in particular find difficulty in providing a final sentence. The well-tried 'And thank you for so patiently listening to me' always goes down well: 'Thank you again for this happy evening' is not original but adequate: and a popular one is 'We look forward to being with you again next year.'

Here, then, are some suggested speeches which can be adapted or added to as the occasion demands. The first two are for the Master's wife:

If any of you should be wondering what is responsible for the strange tapping noise from the top table, I must explain at once that it is caused by my knees knocking together! I am assured that there can be no possible reason for this phenomenon, particularly as ... (my husband) tells me that if there is one quality for which your lodge has been renowned for the past ... years, it is *friendliness*. After listening to ...'s kindly speech proposing the health of the ladies, I am quite certain that that lovely warm feeling still exists.

How pleasant it is to be so enthusiastically welcomed by a company of gentlemen to all of whose *other* meetings women are firmly excluded! On behalf of all the ladies I should like to thank you, Mr President, for inviting us to this most happy event and for giving us such delightful presents. These each of us will treasure as a memento of a very happy evening.

I'm glad my husband is a Mason, and I am happy to accept that the principles of Freemasonry cannot be other than beneficial to the world at large. That sentiment is not intended as an exchange for the flattery in ...'s speech: I really mean it. So once again we thank you for our lovely evening.

This suggestion is on much the same theme:

I wouldn't want to say that I am scared stiff, but I must confess that in rising to address the company, my sensations are not entirely free from fear! You might wonder why this should be so in such a friendly company, and after having heard such a flattering speech. So thank you very much, Mr President and gentlemen, for the enthusiasm with which you honoured the toast to our health. I'm beginning to feel better already!

Thank you, also, for your presents which we shall all regard as a delightful memento of this Ladies' Night. I gather that ..., my husband, is the Worshipful Master of most of you nice men. I should love to see you worshipping him—and I hope you all enjoy it! There was a time, alas long ago, when he used to give me to understand that it was *he* who did the worshipping, and that *I* was the object of the adoration!

But seriously, we are glad to be in the company of such distinguished men, and if you are representative of the whole body of Masons, I can only say that your wives are proud of you. We are greatly enjoying our evening, my knees seem to have quietened down, and we all hope you will invite us again next year.

If the response to the toast is to be, as is not unusual, the first speech the lady has ever made, she might care to try something like this:

In the story of my life, this evening will go down as my most memorable experience. For, believe it or not, I am making my very first speech. By that I mean my very first *public* speech. Like any woman who has been married as long as I have, I've spoken often enough in *private*! Well, haven't we all held forth from time to time? I'm not as bad as one of (husband) ...'s friends who says that his wife talks so much that if *he* were struck dumb it would take *her* a week to discover it!

So let me get down to business, consoled by the thought that after to-night's performance I am unlikely ever to be asked to repeat it. My pleasant duty is to say thank you on behalf of the ladies to ..., the proposer of our toast, for all the nice comfortable and flattering

things he had to say about us. That they were all perfectly true goes without saying. If this had not been so,
you gentlemen would not have toasted us so enthusiastically. Thank you also for our delightful presents which
we shall always treasure as a reminder of a lovely evening. Indeed, I have an idea which the members of the
Lodge might care to consider. It is this, that you might
hold Ladies' Nights in September, October, February and
March (vary months to accord with actual meeting
dates) and have just one Lodge meeting, say, in April.
Just consider what a lot of brain fag you gentlemen
would be saved!

But seriously, Mr President and gentlemen, we are
glad that our husbands are Masons; for although our
knowledge of Freemasonry is small and scrappy, we do
believe that its influence and its good works shine out
in the world at large.

Having said that, I can now sit down and take that
nice long drink which I couldn't have earlier in case I
got my words mixed! Thank you for listening to me.

The responder to the toast to The Ladies need not necessarily be related to the Master, or indeed to any of the
brethren. Her approach in this case will be rather different
from that in the suggestions I have made. Something like
this perhaps:

When I was a little girl I used to go to parties, and there
were two points of etiquette about which my mother
was most insistent. The first was that I should politely
say 'After you' when the cakes were passed round; and
the second was that when leaving I should never omit to
say THANK YOU to my hostess. The observance of the
first generally resulted in my getting the most luscious cakes;
and the polite THANK YOU almost invariably meant
that I was asked again.

I assure you, Mr President, that it is something more
than mere politeness which prompts me to rise to ex-

press the thanks of the ladies for the kindly terms which have been voiced by Mr ... in proposing our health. We appreciate his reminders of our various excellences, and we congratulate him on his powers of observation and penetration!

As one whose knowledge of Freemasonry could be comfortably written on the back of a postage stamp, you will not expect me to show the same knowledge of your members as they obviously have of us. Suffice it to say, therefore, that we cannot visualise a more distinguished, considerate and altogether friendly company than that in which we find ourselves this evening.

I am sorry to learn that your Order is not open to women, because if it *had* been, I, for one, would have been clamouring for admission. I have learned this evening just a little of your many and varied good works, not only in respect of your own members, but also of your charitable concern in many directions. Indeed we have had evidence of this to-night in the delightful presents you have provided for each of us—gifts which we shall treasure as happy reminders of a lovely evening.

In my mother's words then: 'Thank you very much, all you kind gentlemen, for having us!'

The toast to the President or Presiding Officer is of necessity different from that given after a masonic dinner, since a Ladies' Night is not strictly a masonic function. The proposer is severely limited by the fact that masonic allusions as such are taboo, and he must therefore confine himself to the President's personal qualities and interests. Something in the style of the following might find favour:

'Let us now praise famous men' says the Book of Ecclesiasticus. There are degrees of fame, and it is possible that you, Mr President, might be the first to deny that you have a place in any of them. We who are present this evening consider that you are entitled to your measure of fame for the confident and friendly manner in which you are directing the proceedings. To be amicable, considerate and interested in each and every one of us is most commendable, and we all appreciate it.

You might wonder how a man who spends so much of his time on the golf course (or whatever his other interests may be) could be so knowledgeable on other subjects. Ladies and gentlemen, to a (list them as appropriate, such as) chartered accountant, Ex Fleet Air Arm, golfer, traveller and artist, I call upon you to raise your glasses to toast them all in THE PRESIDENT.

CHAPTER FIFTEEN
Finding material

The short speeches which I have provided in previous chapters have seldom contained quotations. This is not because quotations should not be used where they are suitable, but rather that their employment is very much a personal and topical matter. Over many years it has been my practice to pick up odds and ends which I think might be worth repeating when the opportunity arises. Quite often I forget their source. I would recommend the study of the letter pages of the daily press where occasionally a useful bit of wit appears—to be cut out and put away for a while until people have forgotten it. This applies also to the occasional paragraph from 'Peterborough' in the *Daily Telegraph*. He will often be found to have borrowed some of his best bits from local newspapers.

Quotations should be used with a certain amount of care, and should normally be quite short. Like anecdotes, it takes more ingenuity than the job is worth to introduce a quotation and then seek for a reason to bring it in. It is not always necessary to quote the source, although there are certain quotations which would lose their point if the source were not mentioned. Take, for example, the very well known one from Winston Churchill:

> He can best be described as one of those orators who, before they get up, don't know what they are going to say; when they are speaking, don't know what they are saying; and when they have sat down, don't know what they have said.

And for heaven's sake don't produce that with reference to a speaker who has preceded you!

In the matter of your own speeches you might feel like quoting a text from the Apocrypha: 'Let thy speech be short, comprehending much in few words.' And this is a similar one from the Marriage Service in the *Book of Common Prayer*: 'Let him now speak or else forever hereafter hold his peace.'

There is a much-quoted extract from a speech made several years ago by Lord Birkett. It is now so old that perhaps your hearers may not have heard it—or maybe they will have forgotten it: 'I do not object to people looking at their watches when I am speaking: but I strongly object when they start shaking them to make certain that they are still going!'

Like me, everyone has his store, great or small, of sayings accumulated over the years, the source of which he may long since have forgotten. Sometimes they spring to mind unbidden, but most of us can be certain that when we are searching for any particular phrase, it can be relied upon to elude us. A much-quoted sentiment which often comes to my mind, and has proved useful in a humorous after-dinner context occurs (I believe) in the works of an American humorist of the last century: 'The wheel that squeaks the loudest is the one that gets the grease!'

Another one, passed to me in the course of discussion long ago and still useful on occasions is to the effect that 'there are *three* sides to every question—my side, your side, and to hell with it!' Another which comes to mind, and which you might find useful on a Ladies' Night, exhorts you to: 'Always meet your troubles like a man. Blame them on your wife!'

Although you will generally be forgiven for misquoting, there are a number of famous classical quotations which, if not given with complete accuracy, will call down criticism on your head. For example, 'A little *learning* (not knowledge) is a dangerous thing.' Robert Burns' Selkirk Grace not infrequently comes in for some strange versions. This is the correct one:

'Some hae meat, and canna eat,
And some wad eat that want it,
But we hae meat and we can eat,
And sae the Lord be thankit.'

While on the subject of Grace, here is an Elizabethan Grace written in 1588, the year of the Armada, by an ironmonger from Exeter, and used at the jubilee luncheon to our present Queen at Guildhall in 1977:

'God blesse our meate, God guide our waies,
God give us grace our Lord to please,
Lorde longe preserve in peace and healthe
Our gracious Queene Elizabeth.'

A further few lines of Burns which get misquoted come (believe it or not) from a sonnet to a louse:

'O wad some Pow'r the giftie gie us
To see oursels as others see us!
It wad frae mony a blunder free us,
And foolish notion.'

Here is a fairly comprehensive selection of some of the quotations from my own collection. I have, as I have said, forgotten the source of many of them, and I apologise for any inaccuracies. All, I feel, are suitable for retailing after the lodge dinner, and some will be more useful at the Ladies' Night. For ease of reference I have divided them into fairly widely ranging subjects: three of these, in my experience, especially lend themselves to quotation. These are Age, The Ladies, and what I can best describe as Natural Philosophy. So here goes:

Advice

When you have nothing to say, say nothing. (*Charles Colton*)

We know what happens to people who stay in the middle of the road. They get run over. (*Aneurin Bevan*)

It's the overtakers who keep the undertakers.

Be nice to people on your way up, because you may meet them on your way down.

Golden Rule when reading the à la carte menu: If you can't pronounce it you can't afford it.

This is a piece of advice on the subject of speechmaking which is reported to have been given by Winston Churchill to the Prince of Wales: 'If you have an important point to make, don't try to be subtle or clever. Use a pile driver. Hit the point once. Then come back and hit it a second time — a tremendous whack.'

While in the presence of Royalty, this comes from the Duke of Edinburgh: 'The art of being a good guest is to know when to leave.'

No dream comes true until you wake up and go to work.

This comes from a collection of Country Sayings: 'A good scare is worth more to a man than good advice.'

After-dinner speaking

The guests are met, the feast is set. May'st hear the merry din. (Coleridge: *Ancient Mariner*)

The only after-dinner speech of mine that can be relied upon to go down well is when I'm at home, and I turn to my wife and say: 'You leave them, dear. I'll do 'em.'

It usually takes three weeks to make a good impromptu speech. (*Mark Twain*)

Eloquence is what you think you have after five drinks.

Age

I love everything that's old: old friends, old times, old manners, old books, old wines. (*Oliver Goldsmith*)

To me, old age is always fifteen years older than I am (*Bernard Baruch*)

The worst of living is that you get older every day. I am not young enough to know everything. (*Sir James Barrie*)

It's years since I gave a mink coat to anybody except a member of my family. (*A greatly respected judge*)

I prefer old age to its alternative. (*Maurice Chevalier*)

Whenever a man's friends begin to compliment him about looking young, he may be sure that they think he's growing old.

There's one thing to be said for baldness: it's neat!

So often the *good old days* are no more than the result of a bad memory.

By the time you're eighty you've learned everything. All you have to do is to remember it.

Here is another from Maurice Chevalier: The only difference between a man of forty and one of seventy is thirty years of experience.

Age improves wine, compound interest, and nothing else that I can think of.

These are the Three Ages of Man: Youth, Middle Age, and 'You're looking well.'

The late Sir Frank Milton, who was Chief Metropolitan Magistrate, said: 'I am always terrified when a young policeman speaks about "an old lady." She usually turns out to be about 35.'

Here is another bit of wisdom from Henry Ford: Anyone who stops learning is old, whether at twenty or eighty.

Anyone who keeps learning stays young. The greatest
thing in life is to keep your mind young.
Lastly, a lovely bit of verse from Robert Browning:
>   Grow old along with me!
>   The best is yet to be,
>   The last of life, for which the first was made.

Bankers

Mark Twain's definition is much quoted and will often be
found useful. A banker, said he, is a fellow who lends his
umbrella when the sun is shining, and wants it back the
minute it begins to rain.
This comes from the Chairman at an Institute of Bankers
Seminar: Some customers regard their bank manager as
the only obstacle between them and the chance to live
beyond their means.

Bore

A bore is a man who, when you ask him how he is, tells
you.
A bore is a person who talks when you wish him to listen.

Commerce

There is hardly anything in the world that some man cannot make a little worse and sell a little cheaper. (*Ruskin*)

The English

Even in the eighteenth century Samuel Johnson had
observed that when two Englishmen meet, their first talk
is of the weather.
This is Winston Churchill's famous marginal comment on
a certain State document: 'This is the sort of English up
with which I will not put.'

This comes from a speech by the Duke of Edinburgh at a Conference of the English-Speaking Union: 'I include pidgin-English, even though I am referred to in that splendid language as "Fella belong Mrs Queen."'

Correspondence in the *Daily Telegraph* brought out some interesting examples of idiomatic English. Here are some examples: After being knocked down you are laid up; you chop a tree down and then you chop it up. You can't buy butter in a buttery, vests in a vestry or pants in a pantry. When a company wishes to expand they call in a contractor; and however respectable a lady solicitor may be, she can get into serious trouble for soliciting.

This is an epitaph in a Cornish churchyard:
> She as was is gone from we.
> Us as is must go to she.

This is the view of a famous Frenchman: the English are like their own beer: froth on top, dregs at the bottom, the middle excellent.

Fame

After a fellow gets famous it doesn't take long for someone to bob up that used to sit by him at school.

The man who wakes up and finds himself famous hasn't been asleep.

In a letter to Sir Joshua Reynolds in 1771, Samuel Johnson wrote: Every man has a lurking wish to appear considerable in his native place.

Friendship
> From quiet homes and first beginning,
> Out to the undiscovered ends,
> There's nothing worth the wear of winning,
> But laughter and the love of friends.

> (*Hillaire Belloc*)

The social, friendly, honest man,
Whate'er he be,
'Tis he fulfils great Nature's plan,
And none but he.

(Robert Burns: Epistle to Lapraik)

This might be suitable for a little gentle leg-pulling at a Ladies' Night: it comes from G.K. Chesterton. 'A man's friend likes him but leaves him as he is. His wife loves him and is always trying to turn him into somebody else.'

Charles Lamb wrote, I think in his *Essays of Elia*, The greatest pleasure I know is to do a good action by stealth, and to have it found out by accident.

And another wish from Mark Twain: When you *ascend* the hill of prosperity may you not meet a friend.

The Future

The Future is that period of time in which our affairs prosper, our friends are true, and our happiness is assured.

The Future is something which everyone reaches at the rate of sixty minutes an hour, whatever he does, and whoever he is. (C.S. Lewis)

Here is a typical comment from Samuel Johnson: The future is purchased by the present.

Golf

All I've got against Golf is that it takes you so far from the club house. (Eric Linklater)

Golf was defined by the poet Wordsworth as a day spent in a round of strenuous idleness.

The emphasis placed on keeping your eye on the ball is the best proof that Golf originated in Scotland.

Good Intentions

I shall pass through this world but once. If, therefore, there can be any kindness I can show, or any good thing I can do, let me do it now; let me not defer it or neglect it, for I shall not pass this way again. (Several writers have been credited with this.)

Health

Here is another of Henry Ford's priceless aphorisms: Exercise is bunk. If you are healthy you don't need it: if you are sick, you shouldn't take it.

Clement Freud had a not dissimilar idea: If you resolve to give up smoking, drinking and loving, you don't actually *live* longer: it just *seems* longer.

Perhaps Joseph Addison in the 1700's got it right: Health and cheerfulness mutually beget each other.

Ladies

This is the oft-quoted remark of a Victorian lady on a performance of *Antony and Cleopatra*: 'How different, how very different, from the home life of our own dear Queen!'

Has a woman who knew that she was well-dressed ever caught a cold?

Wives, according to Francis Bacon, are young men's mistresses, companions for middle age, and old men's nurses.

Faithless to them though he was, and sometimes cruel, Robert Burns wrote delightfully of the lassies:

> The sweetest hours that e'er I spend
> Are spent among the lassies O.

Two more lovely lines from the same song:

> What signifies the life o' man,
> An' 'twere not for the lassies O.

Or this one:

> Auld Nature swears, the lovely dears,
> Her noblest work she classes O;
> Her prentice han' she tried on man,
> An' *then* she made the lasses O.

A few may perhaps remember a music hall song of the turn of the century which went: 'A man is as old as he's feeling, A woman as old as she looks.'

The essayist, R.W. Emerson, gave it as his opinion that a lady's sense of being well-dressed gives a feeling of inward tranquillity which religion is powerless to bestow.

A diplomat is a man who always remembers a woman's birthday but never remembers her age.

The following, I am told, has been quoted as the considered opinion of a high ranking police officer: 'Give a woman an inch and she'll park a car on it.'

This comes from the Jewish Talmud: 'God did not create woman from man's head that he should command her, nor from his feet that she should be his slave, but rather from his side that she should be near his heart and by his side.'

Behind every successful man there stands an astonished mother-in-law.

One of the difficult tasks in this world is to convince a woman that even a bargain costs money.

This might be of use to end the toast to the ladies: Here's to our wives and sweethearts! May our sweethearts become our wives, and our wives ever remain our sweethearts!

Luck

J. Bronowski's opinion is true, I suppose, of most of us: 'The world is made of people who never quite get into the first team and who just miss the prizes at the Flower Show.'

This one is worth bearing in mind: If at first you *do* succeed, don't take any more chances!

Mixed metaphors

These three are attributed (but with what degree of accuracy I should not like to say) to Sam Goldwyn:
If Roosevelt were alive he'd turn in his grave.
A verbal contract isn't worth the paper it's written on.
You ought to take the bull between the teeth.

Music

It is the best of all trades to make songs, and the second best to sing them. (*Hilaire Belloc*)
This is from the diary of dear Samuel Pepys: Music and women I cannot but give way to, whatever my business is.

Philosophy

Kipling put it this way:
    If you can fill the unforgiving minute
    With sixty seconds' worth of distance run,
    Yours is the earth and everything that's in it,
    And—which is more—you'll be a Man, my son.
The last line was, to my mind, considerably improved by a doctor in *The Lancet*, re-writing it as:
    And a coronary before you're sixty-one.

      This one is sometimes misquoted:
      Two men look out through the same bars:
      One sees the mud, and one the stars.

Genius, according to Thomas Alva Edison, is one-per-cent inspiration and ninety-nine-per-cent perspiration.

A dwarf standing on the shoulders of a giant may see further than the giant himself.

I have found some of the best reasons I ever had for

remaining at the bottom simply by looking at the men at the top. (For goodness sake be careful as to how you use that!)

Never forget that it is only *dead* fish that swim with the stream.

It is reported of the great composer Beethoven that he gently reproved a cocky young man with: 'Please believe that the opposite may also be true.'

Meditation is what we call idleness if we catch anyone else doing it.

A Fool's Paradise is nevertheless a paradise.

There are three essentials to happiness, namely something to do, something to love, and something to hope for.

Rebuke

The great Austrian conductor, Hans Richter (1843–1916) conducted the first British performances of *The Master-singers* and *Tristan* in 1882 and 1884. As a conductor he was a stern disciplinarian. His English was not very good, as is evidenced by this rebuke to a member of the orchestra at rehearsal: 'Your damned nonsense can I stand twice or once, but sometimes always, by God, never!'

The Unknown

Death is, after all, the only universal experience except birth.

This extract from the work of Miss Haskins, a quietly sweet and retiring lady whom I knew years ago, was quoted in a Christmas broadcast by King George VI, and is frequently repeated with greater or less accuracy under the heading of 'The Gate of the Year'. Here it is as the King quoted it: And I said to the man who stood at the gate of the year: 'Give me a light that I may tread safely into the unknown.'

And he replied: 'Go out into the darkness and put your hand into the hand of God. That shall be to you better than a light and safer than a known way.'

Work

Work is the grand cure of all the maladies and miseries that ever beset mankind. (Thomas Carlyle in his Rectorial Address at Edinburgh, 1886.)

Every man's work, whether it be literature or music or pictures or architecture or anything else, is always a portrait of himself. (Samuel Butler, *The Way of all Flesh*)

Youth

This comes from a schoolboy's end-of-term examination paper: 'Nelson was an admiral who commanded the Victory, and died on a plaque which marks the place in the sea where he fell.'

This could have come from the same knowledgeable youngster: 'Florence Nightingale was a woman who used to sing in Berkeley Square.'

The ever youthful Fred Astaire said: 'Old age is like everything else. To make a success of it you've got to start young.'

The young are so busy teaching *us*, that they have no time left to learn.

CHAPTER SIXTEEN

And finally

I propose in this chapter to gather up the fragments that remain. In doing this I shall strive for accuracy in relating some of the interesting and occasionally amusing masonic incidents which find their way into speeches from time to time.

Lady Freemasons

Possibly no story exists in a greater variety of versions than that of the so-called only Lady Freemason. Careful investigation made nearly a hundred years ago shows her to have been the Hon Elizabeth St Leger, the daughter of the 1st Viscount Doneraile. About the year 1710 the meetings of a masonic lodge used to be held in a room in her father's house, the butler acting as tyler. Elizabeth had apparently been taking a nap in the library which adjoined the lodge room, and when she awoke she realised that a meeting must be taking place in the next room. Repairs which had been in progress had resulted in some bricks between the two rooms being carelessly replaced, so that it was no trouble to Elizabeth to remove them and so to get an uninterrupted view of what was going forward.

Apparently the solemn obligation of the initiate convinced her that here was something she ought not to be witnessing. She therefore retreated to the hall where it was obvious to the tyler-cum-butler that the lodge had been the victim of a fair intruder. Elizabeth thereupon screamed and fainted, and the tyler called out her father and brothers who, having seen the unconscious lady, returned to the lodge to discuss what should be done. The brethren decided that, with her consent, she should be initiated. This was accordingly carried out. Elizabeth later became the Hon Mrs Aldworth, and after her death in 1773, Irish Freemasons used to toast the memory of 'Our Sister Aldworth', and her masonic apron is still exhibited.

Mozart

When the occasion calls for some mention of music and masonry, the name of the great composer, Mozart, springs up. Music owes a debt to Freemasonry: for it is possible that if it had not been for the generosity of Brother Michael Puchberg, one of Mozart's masonic brethren, the composer might have died at an even earlier age than 35. Mozart was initiated in 1784, and within four years his desperate financial circumstances led to his pleading for help from Brother Puchberg who did his best again and again. Nor was Puchberg the only brother to be called upon. Although by present-day standards poor Mozart does not stand out as a model Mason, he nevertheless loved the Craft deeply, and composed some very beautiful music for use in the ceremonies. The Masonic Funeral Music is well known, and so is the opera, 'The Magic Flute', the libretto of which is the work of another Mason, Emanuel Schikeneder, and embodies some masonic symbolism.

Tyler

Another early and impecunious Mason was the first Grand Master, Anthony Sayer, who was elected in 1717. He was the senior in a procession of ten Grand Masters at the installation of the Catholic Duke of Norfolk in 1730. Petitions for financial help were made on his behalf in 1724, 1730 and 1741, the last of which resulted in his receiving a donation of two guineas. At the time of his death in the following year the Past Grand Master was Tyler of what is now the Old King's Arms Lodge No 28. Lodge tylers might

care to reflect—not without pride—that among their number was the very first Grand Master.

Free-man

To many the enquiry at their initiation, 'Are you a free
man?' might seem pointless. It stems from an eighteenth
century practice of making men masons while actually in
prison. The colourful revolutionary, John Wilkes, having
fled to France and been outlawed in 1764, returned to
England in 1768 and succeeded in getting himself sent to
parliament. The justiciaries would have none of this and
promptly expelled him from parliament and committed him
to prison. Here in 1769 he was initiated into Masonry.

This seems the more strange since some six years earlier
Captain George Smith, Provincial Grand Master of Kent,
was arraigned before Grand Lodge for making masons in
a clandestine manner in the King's Bench Prison. On this
occasion Grand Lodge held firmly that it was inconsistent
with the principles of Masonry to hold a lodge in any place
of confinement.

Freemasons all

Readers of *Masonic Square* might care to refer to two articles of mine containing details of other Masons, famous
and infamous. Branwell Brontë appears under the title 'The
Pathetic Glory' in the December 1979 issue. Cagliostro,
George Cooke and Charles Dawson are described under
the heading 'Masonic Fakers' in the issue of June, 1984.

Royalty

The connection with Masonry of a succession of kings and
princes has sometimes led to the comment from non-
masons that royal interest in the Craft is probably more
apparent than real. Among the long list of royal Freemasons it is doubtful whether any had as deep an affection

for the Craft as H.M. King George VI. The king took to Masonry with tremendous zeal and enthusiasm. Initiated into the Navy Lodge in 1919, Master in 1921 and Grand Master in 1924 shows pretty rapid progress, but the more human story is of his reception into Scottish Masonry as Duke of York in 1936, when he was received into Lodge Glamis No. 99 at the hands of Brother Beattie, the village postman.

In the same year, and just at the time of the abdication, two days indeed before the press released the story of Mrs Simpson, he was installed Grand Master of Scotland. He made masonic history as the only British sovereign to participate publicly in the observances of the Order, and not to be a mere figurehead. He was inducted as Past Grand Master at the Albert Hall in 1937, and as such he later personally installed three Grand Masters—the Duke of Kent in 1939, Lord Harewood in 1943, and Duke of Devonshire in 1948. Only illness prevented his installing Lord Scarbrough in 1951. Brethren privileged to be present were unanimous in acclaiming the perfection of the work of Most Worshipful Brother His Majesty King George VI.

In his biography of the king, Sir John Wheeler Bennet wrote: 'There was much in Masonry which appealed consciously and deeply to King George: its hierarchic discipline: the dignity and simplicity of its ceremonial, of which he was a knowledgeable student: the simplicity and vitality of its three great tenets of Brotherly Love, Relief and Truth. His belief in the Order became the more apparent to those with whom he conversed about it as the years passed. He was influenced by its symbolism, and the record of his daily life bore witness to his strict adherence to its moral and spiritual precepts.'

There are many references to Freemasonry in the king's diaries, and I feel that quite the most moving one refers to his brother after the abdication. He wrote: 'We parted as Freemasons—and he bowed to me as king.' Philatelists will be familiar with the masonic 3D stamp showing King

George VI's head together with the square and compasses, the trowel, and a dove bearing an olive branch.

Public relations

Occasionally some reference may be required in a speech on the matter of Freemasonry's public relations. The official policy of the Board of General Purposes is as follows:

> The Board takes the view that although Freemasonry is not secret (the only 'secrets' are modes of recognition) it is nevertheless intensely private. The Craft has nothing to hide and certainly nothing to be ashamed of, but seeks to avoid having its affairs investigated by outsiders. It would be able to answer any of the questions likely to be asked, but experience has shown that silence is the best practice: comment or correction only breeds further enquiry and leads to the publicity the Craft seeks to avoid. It respects and does not comment on the attitudes of other organisations, and it is unfortunate that they sometimes appear to be less respectful of the Craft's attitude.

From time to time books are published claiming to disclose the genuine secrets of masonry. This has been going on since the 1700s, and masons are recommended not to be drawn into argument with non-masons on the subject of the contents of such books. It is worth bearing in mind that so well were masonic matters guarded in the past that almost the only evidence we have (unreliable though it may be) of much that our ancient brethren did in the ceremonies is only available from the so-called 'exposures' of the eighteenth century.

In January, 1951, long before the current 'exposure' made its appearance, a curate from a South Coast town contributed an article to a magazine called *THEOLOGY* entitled 'Should a Christian be a Freemason?' He asked for an enquiry, and the Church Assembly in annual session debated a motion that a commission should be appointed to report. Evidence was given to the Assembly by the Rev C.E. Douglas to the effect that for the past 250 years Freemasonry had been one of the most potent factors in building modern civilisation. Although not a Freemason, the Archbishop of York spoke in favour of the Craft, and mentioned the then Archbishop of Canterbury and Lord Scarbrough as members of the Order. The attack was completely unsuccessful, and the Assembly rejected the motion with only one disentient—the curate from the South Coast. Out of all this there came some sensational and wildly inaccurate newspaper articles, and a book called *Darkness Visible*. I was told that by far the greatest demand for the book came from Freemasons!

Origins

It is not unknown for after-dinner speakers to make some reference to the supposed biblical origins of Freemasonry, with perhaps a mention of 'Our Grand Master, King Solomon.' I feel that it should be borne in mind that this legendary history belongs exclusively to the symbolism of the Lodge, and should have no place in the more mundane proceedings of the dinner table. There is no proof that the Craft as we know it originated any earlier in time than the medieval operative masons of Britain. In the words of Pick and Knight's invaluable *Pocket History of Freemasonry*: 'No doubt it incorporated from the earliest times shreds of ritual, folk-lore and even occult elements, of time immemorial antiquity. But it is almost certainly a British product and of British origin.'

Absent Brethren

The toast to Absent Brethren is submitted in most lodges' after-proceedings at 9 o'clock, and is generally known as the 9 o'clock toast. It is given by the Master without any additional words. A masonic writer has suggested that it may take its rise from the utilitarian custom in the eighteenth century of charging all the brethren present for their refreshment at 9 o'clock, when the absence of certain brethren would then be at once apparent. It might be felt that such brethren are nowadays sufficiently brought to mind in the Tyler's Toast which winds up the evening. My purely personal feeling is that the toast to absent brethren provides an opportunity to remember with affection those brethren from among us who have been called to the Grand Lodge Above.

In closing

And finally just a few thoughts on what has gone before. The advice which I have given is based on considerable experience, but it is quite likely that some of the points I have made may not be suitable for the individual *you*. We may be brothers but we are all different, and, as I have said, it is not good in public speaking, or in the more confined and intimate surroundings of masonic after-dinner speaking, to pretend to be something we are not.

I hope that some of the material I have provided will be found to be useful and, possibly, instructive. I have tried to ensure accuracy on certain matters which are prone to inaccurate reporting. I wish I could ensure a standard of correct pronunciation of certain words such as *CON*troversy, Kilo*ME*tre and Ir*REV*ocable, over which the BBC is a frequent offender: but this would be an open invitation to dispute! I can only suggest that if you are accustomed to pronouncing these words and others in a different way, who am I to object?

My hope is that you will have picked up some useful ideas from what I have written, and that you will thereby be enabled to face 'Pray silence for . . .' with the confidence which is bred of preparedness. And the very best of luck to you!